Dr. Tiffany  J. Anderson

Transforming Schools for Excellence: Closing the Achievement Gap

Increasing Accountability
in Charter
and Traditional
Public Schools

outskirtspress
DENVER, COLORADO

Transforming Schools for Excellence: Closing the Achievement Gap
Increasing Accountability in Charter and Traditional Public Schools
All Rights Reserved.
Copyright © 2012 Dr. Tiffany C. Anderson
v2.0

Outskirts Press, Inc.
http://www.outskirtspress.com

ISBN: 978-1-4327-8702-8

Library of Congress Control Number: 2012910795

Outskirts Press and the "OP" logo are trademarks belonging to Outskirts Press, Inc.

PRINTED IN THE UNITED STATES OF AMERICA

Contents

List of Tables and Exercises

Acknowledgments

AS MY STEPS are ordered by the Lord, I would like to first and foremost thank God for blessing me in more ways than I could have possibly dreamed. He gives me peace and strength to do his will. I am so grateful to God for my loving parents who instilled a spiritual foundation in my life, and I thank my parents, Rev. Larry Brown and Dr. Edna Montgomery, as they were my first teachers.

Jeremiah 29:11 states: "'For I know the plans I have for you,' declares the LORD, 'plans to prosper you and not to harm you, plans to give you hope and a future.'" I once heard an educator refer to herself as a missionary of hope, and that reference truly does describe the work of educators who transform schools. Through education, we provide hope to many, and ultimately, we improve the future for all.

I thank God for the opportunity to serve and for guiding me on a journey that has provided hope to other educators, parents, and students. I pray this book uplifts your spirit, energizes your soul, and empowers you with strategies to serve students and provide hope to others by helping them create a better, more prosperous future. I believe that it is God's will that we ensure children succeed, and in doing so, we are also successful.

I am so thankful for those who helped me throughout my journey, and I strive to help others in the same way. As I write about educating children, I must take the time to thank my family. My two beautiful children, Whitney and Chris, make me proud every day. While working on this book, I have relied heavily on my supportive husband, who is equally committed to helping me serve and support families in underserved communities. Thank you, Stanley, for your unconditional love, for the joy you bring me, and for your continuous encouragement.

Finally, I'd like to thank my educational mentors and the educator who gave me my first opportunity in administration. My Aunt Joyce D. Hill, whom I lovingly call Auntiee Dee, and my grandparents Obie and Edna Montgomery insisted I attend graduate school and move into a principal position in a school one block from their home. They saw something in me early in my teaching career that I had yet to discover in myself. My grandmother Edna, whom our family refers to as Ma'Dear, is my source of inspiration in the way she lovingly served others. Her passing in 2009 caused me to reflect on ways I could be of greater service to those in my home state of Missouri.

My other two educational mentors both passed away in 2010. The late Dr. Cleveland Hammonds Jr., who served as my superintendent in St. Louis until 2003, inspired me to have the courage to transform schools. In 1998, he assigned Mrs. Juanita Dogget as my second mentor. She served as a principal in St. Louis for twenty-four years, and many benefited greatly from her wisdom. As a result of Dr. Hammonds giving a young educator an opportunity to be an elementary principal and his willingness to mentor me and assign Mrs. Dogget as a second mentor, I not only transformed the school he appointed me to lead, but I have also gone on to support others in improving achievement in school districts across the country, impacting thousands of children. He taught me how to be a mentor and consultant to other educators. Both Dr. Hammonds and Mrs. Dogget gave me guidance throughout my career as a principal and superintendent. Their lives are examples of true servant leadership, and I thank God for placing them in my life. Without the support of my family and other educators, I would not be the educator I am today. I thank all of them for being a blessing to me.

I've Seen What's Possible

"I am only one, but still I am one. I cannot do everything, but still I can do something; and because I cannot do everything, I will not refuse to do something that I can do."

- Helen Keller

TOO OFTEN, PEOPLE focus their attention on the problems within the education system and neglect to acknowledge the schools and practices that are successful. In my personal and professional life, I've had the privilege of working with and observing wonderful teachers, productive classrooms, and successful schools. As a result, I have seen what is possible, and I know that achievement in every school district can improve. The first step of transformation is recognizing that change and success is possible. This book will not only give you the tools for improvement, but it will also provide a clear path to travel on your own transformational journey that will lead to improved academic performance.

How do I know this? I know what's possible because I have not only seen magnificent change in schools who have moved from failing to succeeding in dramatic ways , but I have also been a change agent who has helped transform schools, resulting in schools performing at the highest levels of the state in which they are located.

I have worked in urban, suburban, and rural school districts ranging from 100% African American and 99% poverty to 1% minority and 10% poverty. I have been a classroom teacher, principal, assistant superintendent, superintendent, and adjunct professor. In each of my various leadership positions, I have been part of a team that has closed the achievement gap and significantly improved overall achievement within my first year in the district. Below is a brief summary of my career experiences thus far:

- I started my career at Lemasters Elementary in Riverview Gardens School District in St. Louis, Missouri. Seventy percent of the students received free or reduced lunch. Each week, I video-taped my lessons and reviewed them to reflect on how I could improve. My goal was to continue to advance my instructional practices in hopes of making my students enthusiastic about learning. I knew that always striving to become better was essential for school improvement. At the end of my first year, my students excelled academically and socially beyond their past performance.
- I continued my teaching career at Robinson Elementary School in the Kirkwood School District, a suburban district that participated in the desegregation program. The achievement gap in Kirkwood was significant. After my first year, student achievement improved, and I was awarded Outstanding Beginning Teacher of the Year.
- After having success in third, fourth, and fifth grade classrooms at Robinson, I created an after-school tutoring program called "Closing the Achievement Gap." This six week program showed that any student with behavior or academic challenges could improve socially and academically.
- In 1998, I became the youngest principal in Missouri; I served as principal of Clark School, a challenging school in St. Louis City that had poor academic scores and consisted of 99% African American students. Clark served 100% free and

reduced lunch students. Because of these challenges, Clark School had six principals in three years. During my five years at Clark, the school transformed from the stereotypical poor-performing, urban school to Clark Accelerated Academy. Within my first two years, we made a 20% gain in moving the majority of our students out of the Below Basic levels of performance on the state assessments, and we created an environment in which the majority of our teaching staff remained for at least four consecutive years.

- In 2001, I graduated from Saint Louis University with my doctoral degree in educational leadership, and I moved into central administrative leadership opportunities. I also served as an adjunct professor for Saint Louis University, and later, I served as an adjunct professor for Radford University in Virginia.

- I became an assistant superintendent in the fourth largest school district in Missouri. That role included addressing all initiatives aimed at closing the achievement gap. To accomplish this, we expanded tutoring sites throughout the city of St. Louis to allow students to participate in tutoring in their neighborhoods, and we exposed students to colleges by taking them to visit different schools and by mentoring them on how to gain admission. Steady improvement began immediately.

- I became the first female and first African American superintendent in Montgomery County Public Schools in Virginia. I was one of the 5% of female school district superintendents in the nation. As superintendent, I visited every school and began an immediate needs assessment of the curriculum, relationships, and pedagogy in the district. By improving these three areas, more schools became accredited each year, and by the 2008-2009 school year, all twenty of the schools in Montgomery County became fully accredited and met AYP standards.

- In 2009, I returned to Missouri and continued leading as an administrator and adjunct professor, resulting in schools across districts improving with over 20% academic gains after one full year.
- In 2012, I was presented with the National ASCD Outstanding Young Educator Honoree Award.

While I've learned many lessons about what works well in improving outcomes for students, I've also learned some difficult lessons from tragedy. I hope that by sharing some of those experiences from the perspective of a principal and superintendent, you will gain some strategies to use when unavoidable challenges and tragedies are presented to you. Even tragedy can lead to lessons of hope that ultimately transform schools for improvement.

Early in my career as a principal in the city of St. Louis, I experienced a student loss that changed me as an educator. On March 6, 2001, I received a call at the start of the school day from the police department asking me to check my attendance roster. Within minutes, we completed an attendance check of our 500 students. Upon informing the police that our fourth grader Rodney McAllister was absent, we learned what we feared most: Rodney, our 10-year-old fourth grader who normally greeted all with a smile and a helping hand, had been killed. He'd been attacked by stray dogs in the park across the street from the school. Through our attendance records and his homework that was still in his pocket, his body was identified.

Amidst community outrage towards his mother who didn't realize he was missing and social service workers who had prior reports on his home life, we struggled to make sense of this senseless tragedy. Through this challenge, our school community found new ways to comfort and educate those we served. We taught lessons on compassion and service without judgment as we addressed Rodney's family with the same love we treated Rodney.

Our entire school grew stronger as a community, and we were

reminded that as educators we must work together to find lessons that make us all stronger when faced with challenges that are hard for students to understand. It also reminded us that part of our role as educators is to model ways to humbly serve and to demonstrate love and forgiveness. By doing so, a culture that reflects the same loving values will blossom.

That same year, after Rodney's memorial service, I began receiving anonymous scarves made by an organization called Save the Children. The scarves, which I continue to wear, remind me of the many students like Rodney and of the importance of our role as educators. If we don't save the children we have been given the privilege to serve, who will?

Our success in ensuring all students have a safe, high quality educational experience is not only an educational issue, but it's also a social justice issue. We must work to provide an equitable education for all students, regardless of where they reside. A student's zip code should not determine the quality of education they receive, and it certainly should not be the factor that limits their ability to be safe or to become a productive, contributing citizen.

The topics addressed in this book illustrate and tackle these disparities in the educational system. Some would argue that impoverished communities with poor performing school systems are even more anxious to provide great schools. They just do not have a clear path on how to make that happen, and their reliance on committed educators is their only hope to improve. This makes the work of effective educators committed to closing the achievement gap even more invaluable.

The statistics on the number of students killed in large city school districts should compel us to take action on improving the school systems located in the urban communities. The quality of the school system is highly correlated to the quality of life in the community. Marian Wright Edelman once shared, "The challenge of social justice is to evoke a sense of community that we need to make our nation a better place, just as we make it a safer place."

It's frightening to reflect on the fact that dozens of students from large public city school systems are slain annually in their own communities. Missouri, the state in which I currently lead schools, has had the highest black homicide rate in the nation since 2008. Most of those deaths have occurred in St. Louis and Kansas City, according to a report from *The Missourian*, which reported on data released from the Violence Policy Center.

Every day I think of Rodney and remember that each moment we have with the youth we are privileged to teach is precious, and we must use it to help them discover their own brilliance and identify ways to improve the community in which they live. We must make every effort to fill students with joy, peace, and hope. The tragedy at Clark also reinforced my beliefs in servant leadership and my commitment to ensuring that as educators, we do everything we can to support the academic, social, and emotional needs of every child we encounter.

In a later chapter, strategies to effectively improve safety in schools as part of the school improvement process will be addressed. Having served as the superintendent of the school district in which the Virginia Tech shooting occurred, our district used many strategies to get through the tragedy. These strategies will help other leaders when faced with unexpected district-wide crises situations.

Throughout this book, I will share with you how our school team transformed schools and the lessons we learned from others, so you too can create change in your school community. Improving student achievement depends on the successful implementation and support in three areas:

- Home and School Relationships
- Pedagogy and Effective Instructional Practices
- Aligned, Standards-Based Curriculum

Within each of these categories falls numerous ways to improve student achievement. You will find that most of the research on effective schools addresses topics that fall within one of these three

categories, and the strategies associated with each of these three areas will enable any educator with a practical approach to have an
immediate impact. Throughout this book, I will address each of these
three areas. In addition, this book will share stories of successful
schools, and it will give you resources to use for school improvement.
Viewing other models of success allows us to see that improvement
is possible and transformation happens in schools across the country
by educators who are just like you. By the end of this book, you will
be empowered with the critical tools necessary to transform schools
and systems in order to eliminate the achievement gap and improve
the communities you serve.

CHAPTER 2

Our Mission as Educators

"It is the supreme art of the teacher to awaken joy in creative expression and knowledge."

\- Albert Einstein

THROUGHOUT HISTORY, ACCESS to education and academic success has been linked to socioeconomic status and race. This inequality creates a cycle of social and economic injustice. This problem was evident in early cultures when the majority of families depended on farming to make a living and children had to stay home to help on the farm instead of attending school. It was also apparent during slavery when black children were not admitted into public schools. Today, the gap between middle-class, white students and poor and minority students continues, but educators can break this cycle.

While poverty and race can impact the way a child learns, it does not decrease a child's ability to succeed. All students, regardless of background and status, can achieve at high levels if given the right tools and opportunities. In order to teach disadvantaged students, we need to understand why they often fall behind in school so we can adjust our methods to help them achieve. This means that educators must have an understanding of poverty and the impact it has on children.

Poverty and Education

Poverty impacts the way children function emotionally, socially, and academically. Low-income students have a higher risk for chronic stressors; they often have health and safety concerns, emotional and social difficulties, and academic struggles (Jensen, 2009). Research shows that low-income students are at greater risk for the following experiences:

- Illness
- Inadequate healthcare
- Divorce
- Eviction
- Living in neighborhoods with high crime rates
- Crowded and unstable living environments
- Depression
- Chemical Dependence
- Teen pregnancy
- Domestic violence and abuse
- Loss of a family member
- Low self-esteem

As a result of these experiences, disadvantaged students typically miss the opportunity to develop stable, healthy relationships with others, and they are forced to focus on surviving rather than being innocent children who can learn and grow like their peers. From the time of infancy, they are usually "behind" their peers in their cognitive and social abilities. While they are born with the same innate traits, such as emotions of grief, enjoyment, hatred, rage, surprise, and fear, as their peers, they often lack the abilities that must be taught by caregivers (Jensen, 2009). These taught emotions include humility, forgiveness, empathy, optimism, compassion, sympathy, patience, shame, cooperation, and gratitude (Jensen, 2009). Students who lack these emotions will have behavioral, social, and academic difficulty because they impact a child's ability to learn and interact with others.

All these factors impact a child's academic success. Students from poverty are more likely to have attendance issues and inappropriate behavior, and they may be more difficult to motivate to succeed in school. These behaviors aren't because the child is unwilling or unable to learn; they are often a result of the experiences and obstacles distracting the child. It is important to remember that not all children in poverty have the same experiences and not all children react in the same way to the obstacles poverty presents. However, for the purpose of this book, the focus is on the general trends, patterns, and common occurrences viewed in schools and confirmed by research.

Consider Maslow's Hierarchy of Needs, which illustrates the stages of growth for all individuals. The first two levels consist of basic needs and security such as shelter, food, water, sleep, safety, and health. For

Table 2.1: Maslow's Hierarchy of Needs

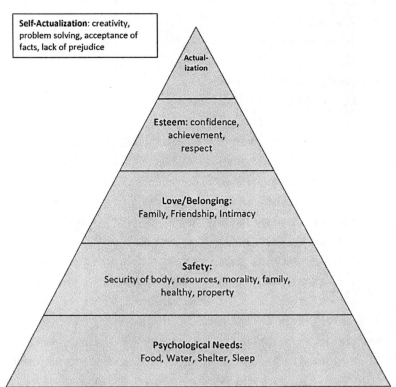

children living in poverty, these basic needs often go unmet. Therefore, children living in poverty often have greater difficulty achieving the highest levels of Maslow's Hierarchy, which include relationships, self-esteem, and academic success. Educators must recognize that these basic needs must be met before learning can take place. This means that schools cannot be just a place of academics, but they must also be a safe, compassionate place that meets the basic needs of children.

Race and Education

Research shows that race is another factor that may impact a child's access to quality educational opportunities, and the two factors, poverty and race, often overlap. The simplest way to understand this reality is by looking at the statistics:

- According to the 2010 Census Report, 46.2 million people in the US are in poverty. This number is up from 43.6 million in 2009, and it is the fourth consecutive annual increase in the number of people in poverty.
- In 2010, 13% of Caucasians, 27.4% of African Americans, 12.1% of Asians, and 26.6% of Hispanics were below the poverty level. There are a significantly higher percentage of African Americans and Hispanics living in poverty compared to other races.
- In 2010, 38.2% of African American children and 32.3% of Hispanic children were living in poverty.

With the current economic struggles, poverty has become the largest factor that contributes to the achievement gap. However, poverty has had a greater impact on minority populations. Therefore, the achievement gap often exemplifies an educational gap between minority students and white students.

Take a look at the two charts on the next pages, which illustrate the achievement gap between African American students and Caucasian students and Hispanic students and Caucasian students in the areas of math and reading. The charts are based on information collected and analyzed by The National Center for Educational Statistics. The data is derived from the results of the 2009 National Assessment of Educational Progress. The following charts show the point-gap between fourth grade minority and white students on the 2009 national assessments.

When studying these charts, it is important to note that research proves that fourth grade literacy is a predictor for future academic success. Therefore, these tables indicate that these minority students may continue to achieve at levels lower than their peers in the future. It is also interesting to note that, according to a program called Learn to Read, over 70% of inmates in American prisons cannot read above a fourth grade level. Research shows that there is a strong link between crime and academic failure. Therefore, it is essential that students master strong reading skills that will not only help them succeed academically but will also give them the opportunity to create a positive, successful life for themselves and decrease their chance of imprisonment and a continued life in poverty.

Table 2.2: Achievement Score Gap in Mathematics for Public School Students at Grade 4, by State or Jurisdiction

Jurisdiction/State	White-Black Achievement Gap (2007)	Hispanic-White Achievement Gap (2009)
Alabama	25	17
Alaska	20	17
Arizona	28	23
Arkansas	28	12
California	29	28
Colorado	26	23
Connecticut	32	26
Delaware	20	18
District of Columbia	54	43
Florida	25	12
Georgia	24	15
Hawaii	14	17

Jurisdiction/State	White-Black Achievement Gap (2007)	Hispanic-White Achievement Gap (2009)
Illinois	32	21
Indiana	25	16
Iowa	21	22
Kansas	26	18
Kentucky	19	14
Louisiana	21	10
Maryland	29	17
Massachusetts	25	26
Michigan	28	16
Minnesota	31	23
Missouri	26	8
Nebraska	33	21
Nevada	23	19
New Hampshire	24	18
New Jersey	23	24
New Mexico	22	21
New York	26	17
North Carolina	27	18
Ohio	25	16
Oklahoma	22	12
Oregon	22	21
Pennsylvania	26	28
Rhode Island	23	28
South Carolina	26	13
South Dakota	24	13
Tennessee	26	14
Texas	23	20
Virginia	23	17
Washington	26	20
Wisconsin	38	22

Source: This chart is adapted from the National Center for Education Statistics reports "How Hispanic and White Students in Public Schools Perform in Mathematics and Reading on the National Assessment of Educational Progress" and "How Black and White Students in Public Schools Perform on the National Assessment of Education Progress."

Table 2.3: Achievement Score Gap in Reading for Public School Students at Grade 4, by State or Jurisdiction

Jurisdiction/State	White-Black Achievement Gap (2007)	Hispanic-White Achievement Gap (2009)
Alabama	26	25
Alaska	22	11
Arizona	17	27
Arkansas	31	22
California	27	31
Colorado	24	32
Connecticut	32	33
Delaware	20	18
District of Columbia	67	49
Florida	24	10
Georgia	5	21
Hawaii	15	12
Illinois	29	28
Indiana	24	24
Iowa	22	16
Kansas	22	19
Kentucky	21	13
Louisiana	26	13
Maryland	28	15
Massachusetts	31	30
Michigan	30	19
Minnesota	33	36
Missouri	26	12
Nebraska	36	21
Nevada	22	23
New Hampshire	14	13
New Jersey	26	24
New Mexico	20	22
New York	26	22
North Carolina	26	26
Ohio	27	15
Oklahoma	19	16

Jurisdiction/State	White-Black Achievement Gap (2007)	Hispanic-White Achievement Gap (2009)
Oregon	25	27
Pennsylvania	33	31
Rhode Island	29	31
South Carolina	26	22
Tennessee	32	22
Texas	25	22
Virginia	20	20
Washington	23	28
Wisconsin	38	25

Source: This chart is adapted from the National Center for Education Statistics reports "How Hispanic and White Students in Public Schools Perform in Mathematics and Reading on the National Assessment of Educational Progress" and "How Black and White Students in Public Schools Perform on the National Assessment of Education Progress."

By studying the charts on the achievement gap, we can see that this is a national problem. It is not limited to a specific geographic region, although some states have higher performance than others. There are many factors that contribute to the high performance in some states compared to the performance of others. It is important to remember that one contributing factor to the varying state performance may be the assessment instrument, which varies in each state. For instance, in Virginia, the state assessment is primarily multiple choice questions, and in Missouri, the assessment is a combination of multiple choice, constructed response, and performance-based questions. This variation in the testing instrument results in scores that are difficult to directly compare. Other contributing factors are the size of the state and the poverty rate; the larger the city and the greater the poverty rate, the more significant the gap in achievement.

Culture and Education

Clearly, poverty and race are two of the major factors contributing to the achievement gap. Cultural barriers, which are often related to race, are also contributing factors. For instance, non-English speaking children may have greater difficulty in the American education system due to language barriers. This does not mean that the children cannot succeed in American schools, but it does mean that teachers must be able to differentiate their teaching in a manner that supports students successfully from various cultural backgrounds. Culturally competent teaching involves including various cultures in the curriculum and training teachers on ways to connect the subject matter to the students' real lives. Improving instructional strategies will be addressed in a later chapter. For now, it is important to first understand and believe that it is the school's responsibility to build relationships with all of their students, and teachers must adapt teaching methods that promote academic success for all students. Students will not learn at high levels from adults they do not trust!

We Can No Longer Ignore the Problem

The No Child Left Behind Act requires all schools, whether urban, suburban, or rural, to address the achievement gap issue. Schools can no longer neglect the students who need them the most, and research shows that these students can achieve at the same levels as their peers. Their ability is not the problem. The way schools educate the diverse populations they serve is the problem, and that is an issue that can be effectively addressed by making some strategic changes immediately.

Closing the gap is not only important for the individual lives of the students but also for our country as whole. By not providing quality education for all students and ensuring that all students succeed to the best of their ability, we are "[underutilizing] human potential" (McKensey 2009). According to a 2009 report produced by the Social Sector Office of McKensey and Company, this underutilization is extremely costly to the US. For instance, the report suggests that by narrowing the gap between low-income students and other students, the country's gross domestic product (GDP) would have been $400 billion to $670 billion higher. Similarly, if the gap between low-performing states and other states had been narrowed, the GDP would have been $425 billion to $700 billion higher. Since GDP refers to the market value of all services and goods produced in the country, these increases could have significantly improved our economy.

Poverty is becoming an increasing issue in the United States, and the need to close the achievement gap is becoming even more important. The McKensey report suggests that if we don't begin to narrow that gap, it will result in a downward spiral for the US economy. It has been proven that academic success is directly related to earnings, health, and incarceration. In order to move our country in a positive direction, we need to improve our education system and tap into the human potential in this country.

As you'll see in the next chapter, there are many schools that are closing these achievement gaps. There are effective ways to overcome this problem. Yes, it will take time and commitment. Yes, it will require dedicated staff, and it requires changing how teaching and learning is approached. But it is possible. With your help, these students can succeed.

CHAPTER 3

Change is Possible

"If there is no struggle, there is no progress."
- Fredrick Douglass

I'VE ALREADY TOLD you a little bit about the success I have been a part of across multiple school districts I've worked within and led. My team in each district has been able to close the achievement gap in multiple settings, and we have helped other educators do the same thing in their own schools. You can also create transformational change, and you can significantly close the achievement gap at your school or across your school district. Listed within this chapter are schools where educational leaders have improved achievement rapidly. If they can do it, you can do it too.

Marva Collins

With her own money, Marva Collins started a school in her home for "unteachable" children. To everyone's disbelief, her students consistently outperformed their peers in the Chicago Public School system.

Kennard Classic Junior Academy

Located in Saint Louis, Missouri, Kennard is the one of few gifted elementary schools in the state. The students come from all races and backgrounds. The school shows that regardless of home environment, culture, or socioeconomic status, all students can excel.

The Charolette Mecklenburg School District

This North Carolina school district has been recognized for closing the achievement gap between Hispanic, African American, and Caucasian students. They outperform 70% of the districts in North Carolina. The district serves 135,000 students, and 675 are free or reduced lunch students. One of their improvement strategies includes moving their most effective school leaders into the lowest performing and highest poverty schools. They recognize that effective leadership is key to improving school performance.

Vann School

This elementary school in Pittsburg, Pennsylvania faces the same issues as any other high-poverty school; it is frequently at risk of being closed and a significant number of students live in the projects. Even with more than 90% of students eligible for free or reduced lunch, the school was awarded a National Blue Ribbon for improved performance and made AYP on multiple occasions.

Mabel Wesley Elementary School

This Houston school shows that dedicated staff and differentiated instruction are the keys to academic success. With all students working above their grade level, Mable Wesley illustrates that middle-class, white students are the not the only ones capable of high academic achievement.

Brazoport Independent School District

Using a business approach, Brazoport was able to increase improvement for all students, especially disadvantaged students, throughout the entire district. After parents demanded to know why the students at Freeport school, which had significantly more disadvantaged students, were not achieving at the same levels as students at the Lake Jackson school, the administration was forced to make major changes. Using a Total Quality Management (TQM) approach, the school was able to increase achievement for all students, decrease the drop-out rate to .1%, and win numerous awards honoring their academic achievements.

Freeport Intermediate School

Freeport Intermediate School is part of the Brazoport Independent School District. During a study by the National Forum and National Association of Secondary School Principals (NASSP) to determine the effectiveness of American middle schools, Freeport Intermediate was the only middle selected as a national model. This was a huge honor for a school with 70% of the student population eligible for free or reduced lunch.

Adlai Stevenson High School

Located in suburban Chicago, this high school is one of only three schools in the entire country to receive the United States Department of Education Blue Ribbon award four times. This school proves that continuous success is possible. In the 1980s, Stevenson's failure rate was over 30% and the annual out-of-school suspension for the entire student population was over 75%. Today, students excel on national assessment tests, and the combined drop-out and failure rate is down from more than 30% to less than 5%.

Boones Mill Elementary School

Located in a rural area of south-central Virginia, the families whose students attend Boones Mill have been hit hard by unemployment. Even with limited resources and students coping with issues at home, Boones Mill has one of the highest test scores in the state.

Los Penasquitos Elementary School

Near San Diego, California, this elementary school serves a diverse student population from both low- and middle-income families and various cultures. In fact, twenty-eight different languages are spoken by the student body. Due to dedicated staff and collaboration, Los Penasquitos is able to help all students achieve at high levels.

Emaniliano Zapata Street Academy

This public high school in Oakland, California serves low-income students and has little technology, yet it earned California's Distinguished School Award in 1990. Emaniliano realizes that a school should not feel or look like a prison. As a result, the students don't act like wild prisoners. Instead, they act like family. Emaniliano shows that success isn't just about the test scores; it is about the school culture and teaching students to be productive members of society.

North Star Academy

A public school in Newark, New Jersey, North Star Academy serves students from a high-poverty neighborhood. The majority of the students are African American. By adapting a data-driven teaching method, the school significantly improved academic achievement, increasing the district average on assessment tests by more than thirty points in every category.

Greater Newark Charter School

Like North Star Academy, Greater Newark Charter School's student population consists of mainly African American students from low-income families. However, the school has been able to significantly improve student achievement and national assessment scores. They have proven that all children can achieve at high levels.

Fort Worthington Elementary School

With 85% of students eligible for free or reduced lunch and 98% of the student population classified as African American, this Baltimore City school struggled to close the achievement gap. By increasing teacher development and assessment practices, this elementary school increased test scores and started to close the achievement gap.

Those are just a few of the many schools achieving at high levels. A comprehensive list of effective schools can be found in the 90/90/90 network by Edtrust or through Doug Reeves' research on 90/90/90 schools. The 90/90/90 network consists of schools characterized as follows: 90% or more of students are eligible for free and reduced lunch, 90% or more of the students are members of an ethnic minority group, and 90% or more of all students met the district or state academic standards in reading or another area (Reeves, 2000). Another link that lists schools that are closing the achievement gap can be found on the State of California's "Closing the Achievement Gap" online resource. The link to this website can be found in the last chapter of this book, which includes titles of recommended readings and websites. In the appendix, you can also find an extensive list of high performing schools.

You may want to use these resources to find high performing schools in your own state. This is a great way to build relationships with other educators and learn from their success. The best way to start creating change in your own school is by studying models of other effective educators. Reach out to the high performing schools in your area, and find out what they are doing to be so successful. In addition, share your success stories with others. The power in our work is how we teach and learn from others so that success can be replicated. The more you can show others what's possible and see for yourself the success that's possible, the more likely it will be that others will be motivated to improve and create ideas to transform their own settings. This is one of the reasons why job-imbedded staff development and action research models work so well with teachers who learn from others.

There is no secret potion or magic formula. You can produce the same results by emulating the characteristics depicted by each of these successful schools. While specific strategies will vary from student to student or school to school, the main ingredients are the same for each success story. By focusing on the success tripod (relationships, pedagogy, and curriculum), you too can improve academic achievement and transform schools for success.

CHAPTER 4

How They Do It

"I have never encountered any children in any group who are not geniuses. There is no mystery on how to teach them. The first thing you do is treat them like human beings and the second thing you do is love them."

- Dr. Asa Hilliard

IF YOU TALK to any educator or student from a high performing school or read any book on education, you will find that there are common characteristics among all successful schools. Sure, each school will have unique ideas and strategies in the way they teach and interact with their students and each book will use different names for the characteristics, but in the end, research shows that each school has the same key components that contribute to their success. Let's take a look at each of those characteristics so you can begin thinking of ways to bring these elements into your own school.

The Subjects

Research shows that high performing schools spend more time on math and communication arts than other schools, and the students are given multiple opportunities to improve their skills in these areas. This is important since most state and national assessments emphasize math and communication arts. Also, these are arguably the two subjects that are most relevant in everyday life, and they are the foundation for other subjects. By spending extended periods of time on these subjects and incorporating other content areas in these subjects, the schools are preparing students for success across content areas.

The Educators

Quality instructional leadership in the classroom, school, and central office is a prevalent theme addressed in research as a primary component of every successful school system. In order to learn, students need great teachers, and the school leadership must be skilled in effective pedagogy and curriculum. Teachers must create a learning environment and encourage analytical thinking, problem solving, and creativity by using teaching methods that are interactive, applicable to everyday life, and challenging. In addition, successful schools have educators that are able to build relationships with the students, and they teach social justice lessons beyond the school curriculum. Effective instructional leadership in the classroom, school office, and central office results in a team that works together to build highly academic school cultures, which lead to high performance.

The Focus

Another common thread among successful schools is a focused vision and/or mission. This can be created for the school as a whole as well as each individual classroom. This mission guides every action of the administration, staff, and student population. Each individual needs to have a sense of purpose and belonging. The mission and vision set the tone for success and can change the way teachers, students, and administrators interact.

The Climate

The climate of the school and classroom is essential to student learning. Children need to feel safe and inspired in order to learn.

There also needs to be a sense of order and purpose, and the staff and administration should have high expectations for every student. In addition, effective schools encourage collaboration, respect, curiosity, experimentation, and reflection. These characteristics are particularly important to students who come from difficult backgrounds such as poverty or unstable households. If you remember Maslow's Hierarchy of Needs from earlier in this book, you know that the prerequisites of security, friendship, trust, respect, and self-confidence must be met before a student can reach the highest level of achievement, which includes the critical skills required for academic success. To review this theory, refer to Table 2.1: Maslow's Hierarchy of needs.

The Self-Check

Effective schools frequently monitor for progress. This includes assessing the students, teachers, and programs. Without this essential step, progress will become stagnant. Schools and teachers need to continuously evaluate themselves and their students to determine what practices and programs are working and what areas need improvement. Successful schools realize that improvement is an ongoing process. We can't simply implement the practices in this book, or use any educational material, and expect spectacular results. We must constantly assess in order to identify problem areas and take steps toward improvement. This process is about figuring out what the challenge areas are and strategically implementing strategies that will work for your students and staff because no two schools and no two students are exactly the same.

The Relationships

There are multiple levels to this category. Schools must create and maintain positive relationships with the families and communities they serve. In addition, teachers and other staff members need to build relationships with the students and each other. This goes back to the idea of creating a climate and culture that encourages trust and collaboration. As a result, students will not only grow academically, but they will also grow socially. As discussed earlier in this book, disadvantaged children often lack the social skills possessed by their peers. Educators need to demonstrate and encourage healthy relationships so students can learn to create and maintain those relationships on their own. This will reduce fighting among students and will encourage team work, both of which will improve academic success and empower students to become problem solvers.

The Experience

In addition to the characteristics described above, effective schools also have an aligned, standards-based curriculum and differentiated, rigorous teaching methods. Common characteristics viewed in high performing school systems include providing multiple opportunities to learn, measuring and increasing time-on-task, and implementing culturally competent practices. Successful schools also realize that every student must be challenged and that content needs to be relatable. Part of the learning process is making associations and transferring skills from one content area to another. In order to do this, teachers need to present the subjects in a manner that is relevant to each individual student. Effective educators realize that no two children are exactly the same, and material and methods must be differentiated to encourage success for all students. School leaders in high performing schools coach teachers to demonstrate these methods, and they assess these areas rather than just focusing on how creative a lesson is being presented.

The Tripod

Right now, you might be thinking "How am I supposed to accomplish all of the things listed in this chapter?" Reading through these characteristics can be overwhelming at first, but if you categorize them into the three areas described earlier, the solutions specific to your school district will become clearer. To create the type of change described in the previous chapter, you need to focus on curriculum, relationships, and pedagogy. By evaluating and improving these three areas, you can develop all of the characteristics discussed in this chapter. As a result, you will significantly improve student achievement.

I have used Ron Ferguson's research from his Tripod project to transform all of the school districts in which I have worked, and others have found that it's a simple way to target problems and solutions in schools. In the following chapters I will address each of these three areas in greater depth, but first, I want you to complete a self-reflection exercise. You cannot start to improve until you know where you currently are. Otherwise, how will you know what needs to change and if your new methods are working? So grab a pen and take a few moments to answer the questions in the self-reflection exercise before moving on.

SELF-REFLECTION EXERCISE 4.1: WHERE AM I NOW?

1) How would you describe your relationship with your students?

_____

_____

_____

_____

_____

2) How would you describe your relationships with the families in your school community?

_____

_____

_____

_____

_____

3) How would you describe your relationship with other teachers and administrators?

_____

_____

_____

_____

_____

4) How much do you know about cultures other than your own?

_____

_____

_____

_____

_____

5) List the top 3-5 issues facing your school or school district in the area of relationships.

_____

_____

_____

_____

_____

6) List the top obstacles facing your school or district in the area of teacher effectiveness?

_____

_____

_____

_____

_____

7) What are the obstacles facing your district in the area of curriculum?

_____

_____

_____

_____

_____

8) How would you describe yourself as an educator? How would others describe you?

_____

_____

_____

_____

_____

9) Identify three high performing schools or districts that you will make time to visit this school year.

_____

_____

_____

_____

_____

10) Can you identify how many students need to improve in each content area to meet your academic target goals? If not, what data can you collect to gain that information?

_____

_____

_____

_____

_____

11) Reflecting on the tripod (relationships, pedagogy, and curriculum), what area do you most need to target first?

_____

_____

_____

_____

_____

12) What are your personal areas of weakness? Do you have team members who complement those areas?

_____

_____

_____

_____

_____

The following survey is a helpful tool in training educators to focus on the area that needs to be addressed first when embarking on school improvement. Once you have assessed your areas of strength and weakness, you may choose to continue reading in one of two ways. You can read the entire book in order and pick strategies from each chapter, or you can skip to the chapter you need to focus on first and return to the others after you begin implementing strategies in the area in which you need the most growth. Note that it is important to improve all three areas in order to create transformational change, but one or two areas may need your urgent attention first.

CHAPTER 5

The Foundation of Success: Relationships and Culture

"It is easier to build strong children than to repair broken men."
- Fredrick Douglas

TAKE A MOMENT to reflect on your childhood. Was there an adult who helped guide and nurture you? Someone who inspired you to be your best and believed in your talents? This could be a teacher, coach, relative, or even a neighbor. Now think about what made that person special. How was that person different than all the other adults in your life?

Most likely, the person was different because he or she listened to you, respected you, and believed in you. That person was probably able to gain your trust and become more than just an adult telling you what to do. That person most likely became your friend and mentor who treated you with respect while encouraging you to be the best person you could be.

Students need educators like that person. They need someone to trust, and they need someone who listens, respects, and believes in them. Research shows that relationships are a key component in high performing schools. Effective teachers and leaders recognize that learning is limited when students don't feel valued and when they don't trust or respect their teachers. Therefore, educators must take the time to build relationships with their students, as well as the students' parents.

Parents' attitudes towards the school and teachers are just as important as the students' feelings, especially in younger grades. It is important that parents value education and encourage their children to succeed, participate, and attend school. Therefore, it is essential that parents be involved in their children's education and support the school and teachers.

Student and parent relationships are directly linked to the school and class culture. In order for educators to gain their students' trust and respect, they must create an environment that encourages these attributes. The school and class culture impact the way students and staff act and communicate. Therefore, it significantly influences the relationships between students, teachers, and parents as well as student achievement.

In order to improve learning, a caring, positive environment must be created. These environments foster cultures in which students and staff feel free to take risks and learn from their mistakes. These schools have a supportive structure in place with distributive leadership.

Creating effective relationships and a nurturing culture don't happen overnight. Both require consistent effort and dedication. However, small changes can make a difference. By implementing simple strategies, we can create transformational change. The key is commitment, perseverance, and sincerity. Students can sense when we genuinely care and when we are just pretending, so it is important for educators to believe that success is possible and to value education and their students by committing to create transformational change.

Before you start implementing these strategies, you need to consider your own intentions and beliefs. Let's begin with a self-reflection exercise before moving on to the practical steps you can use to improve your student, parent, and staff relationships.

SELF-REFLECTION EXERCISE 5.1: RELATIONSHIPS AND EXPECTATIONS

1) What efforts are you currently making to create and maintain relationships with your students, their parents, and your staff?

_____

_____

_____

_____

_____

2) Do you treat all your students equally? Do you believe they can all achieve at high levels?

_____

_____

_____

_____

_____

3) How would you describe your school and classroom culture?

_____

_____

_____

_____

_____

4) What observable actions by students, teachers, and administrators are negatively impacting your school and class culture?

_____

_____

_____

_____

_____

5) What routines have you established with your students?

_____

_____

_____

_____

_____

Now that you have a sense of your strengths and weaknesses, let's take a look at some practical strategies you can use to improve your student, parent, and staff relationships as well as your school and class culture.

Set High Expectations

Research proves that high behavioral and academic expectations are a key element in effective schools. Whether we realize it or not, our expectations influence the way we act towards our students and the teaching strategies we use. Low expectations set students up to fail. High expectations, however, will change the outcomes students are expected to produce and will lead to transformational change and high achievement.

Our expectations not only impact the way we act, but they influence the way our students behave. By setting high expectations, we are motivating our students to succeed at high levels and are encouraging responsible, productive behaviors. This requires us to ignore stereotypes and to view students as individuals rather than groups. If we expect students to behave a certain way, then we limit their potential. But when we eliminate stereotypes, we motivate students to achieve at their highest potential.

It is also important to note that racism is still an issue in our society. Racist attitudes can be subtle or overt and are often the result of cultural upbringings and stereotypical beliefs. As educators, it is important to acknowledge that racist attitudes exist and to make a conscious effort to break them. This means you need to examine your own thinking as well as bring awareness to others. The best way to overcome this issue is cultural awareness and actively seeking ways to promote equity in education through culturally competent practices.

Consider *Martin Luther King Jr. vs. Ann Arbor School Board*, a case about the achievement gap between poor, black students and middle- to upper-class, white students at Martin Luther King Jr. Elementary School. The school was trying to label two-thirds of the African American student population as learning disabled because their reading scores were so low and the students were at risk of being "dangerously illiterate" (Perry 2003). The plaintiff attorney argued there was a cultural barrier in language between the students and staff. The attorney argued that it was the school's responsibility to eliminate the language barrier. The court ruled in favor of the plaintiffs and mandated training for teachers. The teachers needed to use culturally competent practices to improve teaching and learning. This is an example of why cultural competency is so important and how unconscious racism can impact educators' expectations and actions.

Now that you understand why goals and high expectations are so important, let's look at some practical ways to implement goals and high expectations in your school. Remember that no two schools or students are exactly the same. These are guidelines of what has worked in high performing schools, but it is up to you to pick which strategies will work best in your circumstances and to develop new, creative ideas based on the success of others.

- Use SMART goals and encourage teachers to do the same. These goals will require everyone to demonstrate their personal best by working towards achieving the goals. SMART goals list specific, measurable, attainable goals. The resources and timeline that support those goals are also listed. For an example, please visit the appendix located at the end of this book.
- Good enough is not good enough. Promote an attitude of constant improvement, and have students and staff monitor their own data and work towards benchmarks.

- Many high performing schools require students to take grammar courses, and they insist correct grammar is always used when writing and speaking. Therefore, you should promote the use of standard spoken and written English among staff and students. Collaborate with teachers on ways to expand students' vocabulary and the use of proper English. By encouraging staff to use correct grammar, you will set positive examples for the student population. This is important since language is often learned through observation. Hearing and seeing adults and other students speak and write Standard English provides supplemental language instruction.
- Promote learning across all content areas, and monitor progress on benchmark assessments. Encourage teachers to display summary data for each class. Classroom performance should not be hidden.
- Collaborate with teachers regarding signing a professional code of ethics or norms that illustrates how staff will interact. Create the same type of contract with students. The code of ethics or school norms should clearly state what behaviors you expect. A sample code of ethics is included at the end of this book.
- Whenever possible, connect school to the real world and incorporate character education lessons for staff and students.
- Post learning targets and benchmark goals that are challenging but realistic.
- Expect students to understand financial literacy, and integrate this in classes no later than fifth grade.
- Expect students and staff to arrive on time every day. Monitor attendance quarterly, and hold teacher conferences to discuss the results. Likewise, ask teachers to hold parent conferences. Display attendance progress for the school and district. Showing how the school is progressing in all areas will support

the district's focus on district improvements. Each school must reinforce the larger idea that everyone is working together to improve.

- Post expectations and involve student councils in monitoring those expectations. Many schools use character signs along hallways to remind students of various character traits. At a college prep academy that I led, each hall had a name such as "peace hallway" or "respect road," and a street sign was posted in each area. These signs acted as a subtle reminder of the school culture and expectations.
- Urge staff to create signs or charts listing their expectations and the consequences for not meeting them. In the beginning of the school year, they can have students help create these charts or signs. This will encourage teamwork and show students that their input is valued.
- Inform parents of classroom curriculum expectations by ensuring every parent gets a syllabus outlining expectations and the curriculum objectives. Also, post the curriculum and scoring guides on the school website.
- Ensure the curriculum reinforces learning targets and scoring guides for all content areas. Help teachers connect lessons and assignments to those guides. Make sure students are aware of the scoring guides so they have no excuses for not doing the work properly.
- Make sure parents have frequent access to grades through an online accessing system.
- Advise teachers to teach study skills and good work habits. These are not skills that students are born with; they must be taught. If you want your students to succeed, you must equip them with the skills and tools necessary.
- Educate teachers on the RASP strategy for open-ended questions. RASP is an acronym that teaches students to restate, answer using support from the text, and include a personal

connection or opinion. Teaching students multiple strategies to answer questions and to study will give them the tools to be problem solvers and critical thinkers. For a chart illustrating the RASP strategy, visit the appendix.

- Many high performing schools integrate music and rhythmic patterns in teaching mathematics as students learn formulas they must remember. Urge teachers to create or learn these techniques.

- Routinely take time to measure student progress and set new goals. Remember, these should be SMART goals. Be sure to celebrate achievements and effort.

- Require staff to routinely inform students of their grades and require all teachers to write comments on report cards so specific areas are highlighted so improvement and progress can be monitored. Many schools make the mistake of only informing the parent about students' grades, or they let online systems do the work if parents or students wish to know the grades. However, high performing schools hold student conferences frequently in an effort to develop lifelong learners who are accountable for their own education and progress. This should begin at an early age. Holding student-teacher conferences empowers students to set up a plan for self-improvement. This is also the time to identify achievement obstacles that staff can help remove. This practice demonstrates that you care about their success and are willing to help them succeed.

- Ensure students have the tools to complete homework at home. Many high poverty schools do not give textbooks to take home due to the fears that students will lose them. The best way to teach responsibly and to demonstrate trust is to allow students to illustrate responsible behaviors and to hold them accountable as you provide them with resources. It's equally important to provide high expectations with support.

As an example, you may want to encourage teachers to allow time for students to work on homework in class. Many students living in poverty have tremendous responsibility outside of the classroom, and finding time and a quiet place to complete homework can be difficult. While students may not articulate challenges, advise teachers to demonstrate an attitude of understanding while maintaining high expectations with support.

- Support wellness initiatives for students and staff. Having a good balance in life often leads to better camaraderie and student achievement.

- Provide accessible and engaging tutoring services to students who need extra time and support. It is important to ensure students are not missing key instruction during the school day to be tutored in other instructional areas. Therefore, it's important to identify creative ways to extend learning.

- Enlighten teachers and students on the benefits of academic success. Students need to understand why education is so important. This will motivate them to succeed. According to the authors of *Young, Gifted, and Black* (2003), since the time of slavery until the time of the Civil Rights movement, African Americans were motivated to learn because it asserted their freedom and humanity. It was also an act of liberation that prepared them to lead their people. The book suggests that we need to tap into these desires to motivate minority and poor children in schools. We need to show them that education gives them the opportunity to break free from their circumstances and create change in their lives and communities. A good test grade is not motivational enough for most students; we need to show them the lasting impact of academic success.

Create a Culture that Promotes Learning

An effective school culture makes students feel safe and valued. It provides order and structure, and it fosters trust and respect. As a result, students and staff are inspired and motivated, and they learn to work together.

Think about the positive behaviors you expect in your personal community and from your own family. Those are the same characteristics that you should promote in schools that aspire to be a community-centered environment. It is important to remember that you cannot create a culture overnight. The school culture is the result of a school community working together in ways that clearly promote the beliefs the school supports. This takes continuous effort and dedication. Many schools use a school-wide retreat to begin sharing beliefs and to initiate the hard work of addressing school culture, and they revisit these beliefs and vision for the school routinely to monitor progress and make changes as necessary.

In order to create a culture of high expectations, you cannot implement these strategies for a short period of time and then abandon them and expect to create a culture that promotes high achievement. Instead, you must implement consistent behaviors in your school system that continuously promote the values and behaviors that support high expectations. Effective schools hold each other accountable through monitoring, observing, and having team meetings focused on data and aspects of the school culture.

While the characteristics of high performing schools are similar, the strategies often differ. The approach administrators use must be personalized to meet the needs of the communities they serve. As an example, in one district, I expected parents to attend report card meetings routinely, but they didn't. Therefore, we began having parents sign a contract committing to specific behaviors, and we listed support systems to reinforce contracts. For instance, a support may have included a parent conference during a home visit to discuss the expectations that were not met.

While it is important to have high expectations, it is equally important to provide support that helps people meet those expectations. To further support the families in the above example, we began giving groceries to families who met the expectations. We used a grant and philanthropic support to fund the initiative. Parental involvement significantly increased. These strategies worked because they specifically targeted the needs and obstacles of our school's students, parents, and staff. To create transformational change in your own school, you too need to assess your school's needs and implement strategies that will provide support and foster growth in your school community. Here are ways to start creating a positive culture in your school and classrooms.

- Teach lessons on safety and security.
- Make it clear to your students that they are safe at your school by addressing behaviors that threaten safety and security immediately.
- Don't tolerate bullying and verbal abuse.
- Teach conflict resolution skills.
- Use unavoidable tragedies as opportunities to build strength, acceptance, and community. For example, you may recall the tragedy I experienced as a principal early in my career in which our fourth grade student Rodney was killed by stray dogs. After the incident, our students created a memorial that still stands in the park where the incident occurred. We taught our students about civic leadership and community responsibility by rallying for a stray dog law, which was passed the same year as the incident. Watching Rodney's best friend, Devon Gleason, stand next to the mayor as he signed the law was one of the most moving moments in my career; it reminded me that perseverance produces character. Students will have to endure challenges, and it's essential that teachers give students the tools to get through such tragedies and become

better people because of them. We can't avoid all of the bad things in life, but we can turn those tragedies into teachable moments and use our emotions to fuel great change.

- Teach self-discipline. This is a key characteristic of high performing students, but it is not an innate trait. It is a characteristic you can teach your students to improve their academic and social achievement.
- Create a school-wide management system. Students need to learn that actions have consequences and rewards. Rather than focusing on punitive measures to change behavior, you should reinforce positive behaviors. Highlight successes, have alternative instructional models in place within the school to keep students in school when they are suspended, implement strategies from programs such as Positive Behavior Support or Love and Logic, execute procedures for reporting poor behaviors, and train staff on structured, effective discipline techniques. A valuable strategy includes having new teachers observe teachers who have effective classroom management. Also remember that the school sets the tone, and it will be essential for supporting teachers in implementing a similar tone in their own classrooms. Teachers must view themselves as the solution to problems rather than giving their authority and control to other adults and administrators when there are issues.
- Begin the school year with meet and greet activities that allow you to familiarize yourself with the families and demonstrate that you are interested in their concerns. Encourage teachers to do the same and to teach students socialization skills. When students enter the school, be visible and interact with them.
- Use familial language when referring to the school. Always use the word "our" to make students feel like part of a community.
- Personalize the curriculum by using culturally relevant material, and train teachers on culturally relevant teaching strategies. Avoid using books and other materials that aren't relatable. In one school, we personalized our message to

students daily by sharing a song that related to something the school was involved with or related to a character trait. We followed the first few seconds of the song on the intercom with student highlights and information they were interested in hearing about. This led to videotaping announcements for the school, which led to classrooms incorporating their own announcements and success bulletin boards. Everything you do has a ripple effect, so your actions will influence those of other educators. It also important to remember that personality is imperative. You want to create a culture that highlights your students' and staffs' interests and personalities. You don't want to simply copy what has worked for others.

- Encourage teachers to include current events in classroom discussions and make lessons relevant to current societal issues. Also, advise teachers not to force their opinions on the students. Instead, ask the students' thoughts on the events and issues.

- Implement routines. How should students enter the school and classrooms? Where do they put their belongings? What do they do once they are in their seats? How should they transition between classes or subjects? Setting these expectations as a school allows for consistent uniformity in practices. In a school that I led, a teacher created a system in which students earned privileges in a systemic way. Teachers taught other staff members the method and at the start of the year, the entire school used this system to transform our halls and cafeteria. We did learn that this same system could not easily be replicated in other schools because those teachers did not create the system or, as a result, buy in to it. Remember, every school is different, and the school community must be vested in the improvement.

- Write a mission and/or vision statement. Display this for all of the students to see.

- Train employees on the importance of school and class culture.
- Be the change you want to see. Act in the manner you want your students to behave. Children and adults need role models to learn from.
- Make learning fun. Encourage teachers to incorporate games, music, dance, theatre, movies, humor, and surprise. This will make students more enthusiastic about learning and will show them that you care. It will also give them the opportunity to showcase their talents and personalities.
- Take a break to stretch and move. Physical activity can help reduce students' stress and improve concentration. Integrate physical activity in classroom lessons.
- Educate students on healthy living. In order for children to perform to the best of their ability, they need to be healthy. This includes eating properly, exercising, getting adequate sleep, and coping with stress.
- Acknowledge different learning styles and require teachers to include options for assignments that allow students to use their talents such as acting, drawing, playing instruments, writing, or building.
- Explain yourself. Tell students and staff the rationale for certain non-negotiable practices.
- Don't be a stranger. Tell your students and staff a little bit about yourself and your life, and learn a little about theirs. Often staff retreats promote this. Additionally, staff web pages and staff introduction boards for families can accomplish this.
- Promote self-reflection and personal growth. Encourage teachers to use self-reflection to assess their own strengths and weaknesses and measure their personal growth as well as teach their students how to reflect on their personal strengths, weaknesses, growth, and accomplishments. Also, monitor

yourself. At least weekly, consider what is working and what needs improvement.

- Ask for feedback. Students and teachers like to be heard. Find out their opinions on the content and instruction and actually take their suggestions into consideration. This is invaluable information that can help you improve your approach to education and address areas of weakness in your school.
- Let students help make decisions and give them options.
- Suggest that teachers keep a locked note box on their desk, and allow students to deposit notes about issues they are having inside or outside of school.
- Listen. Find out what is going on in the lives of those you serve. In many districts, after learning about a situation a staff member was addressing, our district provided supports to help the staff member get through specific circumstances. It let them know our school community cared about them personally.
- Encourage teachers to schedule class meetings. They should use this time to discuss problems inside or outside of the classroom. This is especially important in high-poverty schools because children living in poverty often lack strong relationships and coping skills. This shows that the teachers care about their students' thoughts, opinions, and concerns, and it teaches students problem solving and coping skills.
- Keep snacks available. Research shows that students who eat breakfast perform better in school. Don't let your students start the day off hungry.
- Have a counselor or social worker go to the classrooms and give lessons on topics the students are dealing with. Also, suggest that the counselor create a system that encourages students to admit when they need to speak with someone. Often, students are embarrassed or afraid of asking for this service, so take the pressure off by making it easy for them to seek help.

Encourage Parental Involvement

During my experiences in leadership positions, I've witnessed the impact positive parent-teacher relationships can have on students' achievement. This is particularly important in areas with high poverty. As we discussed earlier in this book, children's home environments have a major impact on their academic and social success. By building positive home relationships, schools can reduce obstacles that are preventing children from achieving at high levels, and subsequently, they can improve parents' attitudes towards school. Here are some practical tips aimed at removing obstacles for families I've used in the schools.

- Support parent education programs and assist in giving families access to such programs when possible. In areas of high poverty, helping a parent receive a GED can greatly improve the quality of life for the children and thus reduce some of the potential barriers to education.

- Employ a social worker. Educators are only qualified to provide so much emotional support. Some situations require the professional expertise of a social worker, so have one on staff to handle such situations. Make sure students and parents know that the social worker is available to help them.

- Barter for parental involvement. At one school I worked at, we allowed parents to wash their laundry at the school if they volunteered in their child's classroom. We required one hour for every load washed and only permitted parents to wash one load per day. This significantly increased routine parental involvement in the classrooms.

- Work with community members to offer free services to your school's families. This could include medical and mental health services as well as tutoring. Also, collect items such as books, canned foods, and winter jackets for families in need.

- Make parental events convenient. It can be difficult for working parents to attend meetings and events, so make the times and locations as opportune as possible.

- Be visible. Make home visits and participate in activities in the school and neighborhood. Show that you are always available and that you truly care about the community you serve.
- Talk to parents. Find out what their concerns and struggles are. Ask what programs or services would make their lives easier.
- Share ideas with parents on how to help students at home. What activities can they do with their child to improve their reading and/or math skills? What can they do to improve the student's study skills? There are many parents that want to see their children succeed, but they don't always know how to help them get there.
- Create a parent leadership team consisting of parents who want to be involved. This team can help plan ways to address school and community issues and to recruit more parents.
- Host speakers on topics of interest to your community.
- Send home short, weekly newsletters through various venues such as online postings, email list servers, distribution through the community centers, and by sending it home with students. This will help to keep parents informed.
- Provide a list of free resources. Parents might not be willing to ask for this information, so provide it to everyone to avoid embarrassing anyone.
- Call or send notes home when students do something good. It's a nice change from the notes or calls for problems at school, and it shows that you care about the students' success.

Build Relationships with Other Staff Members

In addition to building positive relationships with parents and students, it is important that staff members create and maintain effective relationships. This promotes teamwork and collaboration, which can improve student achievement. It also provides a positive example for the students. The relationships among staff members can enhance or undermine the school culture. By encouraging relationship building among staff members, you are creating a strong foundation on which to build an effective school community. These are just a few ways you can encourage relationship building among staff members.

- Plan social opportunities for staff and for families. This could be a weekly or monthly breakfast, lunch, or dinner. It could also be an occasional outing such as participating in a charity event or hosting a BBQ. The key is to get the staff together in a casual environment that allows everyone to connect on a more personal level.
- Provide positive feedback and acknowledge accomplishments. Compliment staff members when you are impressed by a lesson or achievement. Tell others about the impressive contributions your staff members are making.
- Share ideas. Find out what other teachers are doing in their classrooms as well as how other educational leaders are taking steps towards transformational change. Share these stories with your staff members. Discuss both successes and struggles, but focus on positive stories rather than obstacles.
- Educate staff members on societal issues that impact your school such as poverty or gang involvement. Share examples of high performing schools who've overcome similar situations and students who've made significant improvement. Hearing each other's stories and sharing information inspires people to create transformational change and promotes bonding opportunities.
- Show your staff you care by investing in them. Provide training and time to plan team building activities. Let them know that you support their efforts.
- Talk to your staff members. Find out what is going on in their personal and professional life. What do they need to better serve the students?
- Set up staff committees to address school issues such as safety and academic achievement.

Why Relationships are Important

Research shows that positive relationships and stable environments are essential for healthy social and emotional growth, both of which impact a child's ability to succeed in the classroom and real world. As we discussed earlier, children living in poverty often lack these positive relationships and stable environments. Since we know that poverty is one of the main underlining factors that contribute to the achievement gap, it is important that we address the need for positive relationships and stable environments within school communities. By setting high expectations, developing relationships, and creating a strong school culture, we can improve achievement for all students, especially those who are often left behind.

It is up to educators to build and demonstrate positive relationships among students, staff, and parents and to establish a culture that reflects safety, trust, respect, and order. Research shows that this will significantly improve academic and social achievement. Some of the results of strong relationships include:

- A change in students' attitudes towards learning and their ability to succeed
- Reduced attendance and behavioral issues
- Higher grades and assessment scores
- Better relationships with peers and family members

Creating a Learning Community

We are all learners, and we all have the power to stimulate others to learn and grow in powerful ways. To create transformational change, you need to challenge yourself to seek ways to promote learning while also becoming a student yourself. Excellent educators are always on a journey of continuous improvement. Engaging everyone in the learning process increases the learning aptitude for the entire school community. Professional Learning Communities (PLC) is a process in which schools and districts focus on student achievement in a systematic way. Simplistically put, PLCs focus on three main areas:

- Achievement – Schools identify clear, high achievement goals and align practices in a measurable and attainable way to reach the high achievement levels that are set.
- Teaching – Based on analyzing assessment results, teachers adjust instructional practices, create lesson plans collaboratively, and develop common assessments.
- Collaboration – The school community wants to know that you hear and see them and that their voices matter. By collaborating in an instructionally focused manner, this need can be addressed in a way that causes the school to significantly increase achievement levels. The collaboration through PLCs is focused on professional dialogue, setting achievement goals, analyzing assessment results, and identifying and discussing best practices.

Given the three main areas of focus above, it stands to reason that schools, central offices, school boards, and the community could work as a district professional learning community that uses the PLC principles as the core systematic process for continuous improvement. Imagine how powerful and sustainable school improvement and high achievement would be if every segment of the district modeled effective professional learning communities.

To demonstrate this possibility, let's examine what roles various stakeholders would carry out if PLCs were integrated at every level. The principal's role in a PLC ensures that the school becomes a learning community that engages the students, teachers, parents, and community members in the learning process and in collaborative dialogue on student achievement, which is the focus of PLCs. The principal is the instructional leader that keeps the entire school community concentrated on student achievement. Therefore, even the PTA would be focused on student achievement instead of fundraising and school events.

Now, let's look at the superintendent and school board's role in PLCs. In order to make substantial change, the PLC needs to begin at the superintendent and school board level. The school boards' constant focus needs to be on student achievement, and if the board interacts as a learning community focused on these goals and results, the ripple effect will be a strong achievement focus throughout all of the schools. The district goals should address concrete student achievement results, requiring each school to also have, as a natural focus, the same goals. In cases in which school board members are on committees, which often occurs in larger districts, the committees will also focus on these achievement goals rather operational goals, which are the usual concentration. Content areas are rarely the focus for school board committee work, but if they were, a greater understanding of instruction would be promoted.

It is difficult for schools to address achievement goals when a board has motivations that do not clearly align with student achievement, and subsequently, it pulls the school in multiple directions. Similarly, a board and superintendent who believe in building a learning community will set aside time for essential PLC tasks such collaborative planning. If collaboration time cannot be built into the calendar, creative strategies, such as freeing up staff during the school day by using substitutes or teaching assistants, must be considered. When I joined a district as Chief Academic Officer, we immediately recognized that time for professional development was not in the calendar. Therefore, we assigned certified substitutes to core content areas as we trained grade levels and departments. This example is a reminder that challenges educators to think creatively. Challenges do not have to be barriers but can become opportunities to show others what's possible. Dream big, think big, and be prepared to make every challenge an opportunity to move your school to the next level.

The power behind professional learning communities is that it is a process, not a program. If you take time to instill effective processes that become part of the organization and are ongoing, student learning outcomes will excel naturally. No program will be a silver bullet to address poor achievement, and programs and leaders come and go. Therefore, schools must not be dependent on individuals and programs for sustainable improvement. A systematic process in which people are collaborating together for self-empowerment and development and for the improvement of others will be what it takes to transform organizations in sustainable ways.

According to the authors of *Revisiting Professional Learning Communities at Work: New Insights for Improving Schools (2008)*, PLCs are "the most promising strategy for sustained, substantive school improvement." Therefore, it is essential that educators make the transition from traditional schools to professional learning communities. Traditional schooling no longer works. Every school district needs to make changes to become a PLC. For more information on PLCs, I highly recommend *Revisiting Professional Learning Communities at Work: New Insights for Improving Schools* by Richard DuFour, Rebecca DuFour, and Robert Eaker.

Now that you have practical strategies to implement, let's revisit your self-reflection exercise. Take a few moments to read your answers in the beginning of this chapter. Then, use the information you just read to complete the next exercise.

SELF-REFLECTION EXERCISE 5.2: IMPROVING RELATIONSHIPS AND CULTURE

1) List 3-5 strategies you will implement to improve relationships with your students.

_____

_____

_____

_____

2) List 3-5 strategies you will implement to improve relationships with parents.

_____

_____

_____

_____

_____

3) List 3-5 strategies you will implement to improve relationships with staff members.

_____

_____

_____

_____

_____

4) Describe your ideal class and/or school culture.

_____

_____

_____

_____

_____

5) List 3-5 strategies you will implement to improve your school or classroom culture.

_____

_____

_____

_____

6) List 3-5 people you will share this information with.

_____

_____

_____

_____

_____

7) Summarize one success story (either at your school or another
    school) that inspires you.

_____

_____

_____

_____

_____

Now, copy this page and hang your answers somewhere you will
see them every day. This will remind you of your goals and motivate you to create transformational change even on difficult days.
Incremental change throughout the year can lead to schools that are
transformed into high performing learning environments.

CHAPTER 6

The Importance of Instructional Leadership

"He who opens a school door, closes a prison."

- Victor Hugo

A CHILD IS impacted by factors outside of the school's control, such as socioeconomic status and parental relationships, but schools have the ability to reduce the barriers to education caused by those circumstances. Therefore, educators can help all children succeed regardless of their home obstacles.

Perhaps the most important characteristic of effective schools is instructional leadership. This means that schools not only have great teachers who improve students' academic achievements but also great leaders who support those teachers and students. To close the achievement gap, schools must hire, train, and retain quality teachers as well as exceptional leaders. The success of all the other elements in this book, such as building relationships and culture, writing standards-based curriculum, and monitoring students and staff, all depend on the effectiveness of the teachers and leaders. Without dedicated staff and leaders, the strategies in this book are simply ideas that have worked for other schools and teachers. The people who are dedicated to the school's success will make these strategies work and ultimately improve student achievement and close the achievement gap.

Not only do teachers and leaders impact the success of these strategies, but they have the power to increase or decrease student improvement. In fact, research shows that student achievement is directly linked to the effectiveness of the teacher. For instance, teachers in the 85th percentile of teacher quality, which means they are in the top 15 percent of all teachers, are expected to move their students up more than 8 percentile rankings in one school year (Weber 2010). In addition, highly effective teachers can get an entire year's worth of additional learning out of their students compared to less effective teachers in the same school (Weber 2010). Therefore, it is extremely important that schools hire and retain quality teachers. In addition, they must train mediocre teachers to become more effective.

According to the top selling education book *Waiting for Superman*, it is estimated that having three to four years of top quality teachers in a row could generally overcome the average achievement gap between low-income students and other students (Weber 2010). Therefore, it can be concluded that repeated exposure to effective teachers could also close the achievement gap between minority and white students. *Waiting for Superman*, however, points out that one year with a good teacher followed by a year with a bad teacher can cancel out the benefits of quality teaching for an average student (Weber 2010). Therefore, one quality teacher in a school is not enough. School leaders must commit themselves to hiring, training, and retaining as many effective teachers as possible in order to continuously improve student achievement.

Improving Teacher Effectiveness

So what is an effective teacher? Simply put, an effective teacher is one who consistently gets large gains in student learning, while an ineffective teacher gets small or no gains in student learning. Unfortunately, there is no exact model for an effective teacher. Since teachers are simply humans dedicated to educating and improving the lives of children, every effective teacher is unique. There is no magic checklist to becoming an effective teacher. It is all about figuring out what worked for others and then adopting those skills to mesh with your personality and circumstances. Therefore, the best way to become or identify quality teachers is observation. Study those who have proven they are effective as well as those who need improvement. Look at what the effective teacher is doing versus what the mediocre teacher is doing. Then, apply these techniques to your own classroom or teach them to your staff.

While there is no magic formula for becoming an effective teacher, there are similarities among most quality teachers. The manner in which these techniques and characteristics are used is unique to each individual educator, but the impact each has on student achievement has been proven by research and hands-on experience. Here are strategies and characteristics that you can share with your staff to improve teaching quality.

- Customize lessons to accommodate various skill levels, learning styles, and interests. For instance, some students are visual learners while others are hands-on learners. Therefore, you should consider these learning styles when creating lessons and assignments. Another idea is to offer multiple books at different reading levels on the same subject to modify the lesson for various skill levels.
- Make lessons applicable to the real world. For instance, if you are teaching a lesson on persuasive writing, have students write letters to a real person or entity such as a politician or newspaper, and then mail the letters. You could also create a classroom court to explain the judicial system, or relate math to everyday tasks such as grocery shopping or balancing a checkbook.
- Use a hook to get students interested in learning. For instance, you could begin a poetry lesson by asking students to bring in the lyrics to their favorite song, or you could begin a science

lesson with alarming statistics about the environment or the impact of obesity on individuals' health.

- Provide students with the tools to succeed. This could be equipment such as rulers and compasses for a math lesson or a chart with the proofreading tools for a grammar lesson.

- Challenge the students. Never underestimate what a child is capable of learning and doing. Students can sense when the content is being watered down, and this can negatively impact their self-esteem and desire to learn. Instead, constantly challenge your students to take their thinking and learning to the next level.

- Provide personal attention. Acknowledge each student as an individual, and make an effort to build a relationship with each one. Take time to talk to students and work with them individually.

- Make yourself available for extra help when needed. Everyone learns at a different pace. If a student needs extra help, make time before, during, or after school to assist the student. If you are unable to provide extra support, make sure the student has access to resources such as tutoring.

- Research, research, research. Read books on education. Attend seminars. Talk to other educators. Find out what is working at other schools, and use your research to implement data-based best practices.

- Continue to learn. Education is an ongoing process. You can also improve your skills and learn new information. Take advantage of professional development opportunities, and visit effective schools. This is the best way to become a better teacher.

- Plan ahead. The old cliché "Fail to plan, plan to fail" is a motto every teacher should live by. Teachers need to create lesson plans and have backup plans. The more you plan ahead, the more efficiently you can run your classroom.

- Be willing to take a detour. While planning ahead is essential, quality teachers accept that things don't always go as planned. When you see an opportunity to expand a lesson or you need to spend more time on a topic, be willing to think on your toes and change your plans.

- Decorate your classroom to reflect your school and class culture and to promote learning. Include displays related to the content and related vocabulary you are teaching. Show off students' work and interests.

- Give students hope and confidence. This is especially important for low-income students who may lack these emotions. Students need to believe they can succeed now and in the future, so demonstrate the positive impacts that education can have on one's future and frequently acknowledge and celebrate students' efforts and achievements. For instance, I have taken students on college visits to show them the possibilities that await them, and our school team has assisted them with preparing for and applying to various colleges because we knew that they are capable of getting accepted and achieving at high levels once they are there. Not every student believes they are capable of attending college or understands the importance education has on one's future, so it is up to you to show them. According to an article on the achievement gap in *Educational Leadership*, only 15% of African Americans earn at least a bachelor's degree compared to 29% of Caucasians (Kirst 2004). By helping minority students with the college process, we can change this statistic.

- Include physical activity. As discussed in the previous chapter, physical activity improves concentration and reduces stress.

- Make the content relevant and interesting. Look for ways to connect the content to issues or topics important to the students. Use the content to help students come up with solutions to these issues. Some ideas include obesity, environmental issues, political issues, bullying, eating disorders, and substance abuse.

- Include materials and point of views from various cultures. Effective teachers recognize that cultural practices influence students' thinking inside and outside of school. By using culturally responsive strategies, teachers are recognizing and respecting students' identities and backgrounds as meaningful sources.

- Acknowledge that errors are part of the learning process. Admit and correct the mistakes you make. Show students and staff that everyone slips up, and demonstrate how to overcome and fix errors.

- Include problem solving skills in lessons. Have students figure out what information they need to solve the problem, or as a class discuss, how to handle a specific situation.

- Require students to justify and explain their answers. Teach them to use evidence from the lesson to support their response. For instance, if a student says the theme of a book is "Never give up," ask them to identify specific parts of the book that illustrate that theme.

- Teach students to transfer skills learned in one content area to another. For instance, demonstrate how the scientific method can be applied to other subjects to make educated guesses.

- Encourage teamwork and monitor engagement levels in every lesson. Let students work in groups or as a class, and assign group projects that allow students to use different talents and skills.

- Develop students' character and talents. Education is about more than math, science, history, and language arts. Schools are meant to prepare students to be productive citizens. Effective teachers teach lessons beyond the school curriculum. They teach life lessons about trust, respect, leadership, and responsibility, and they encourage students to become the best version of themselves. They give students the confidence to pursue their passions and talents whether they are academic pursuits such as mathematics, athletic pursuits such as football, or artistic pursuits such as dance.

- Keep an eye on your pace. Pace your lessons to ensure constant engagement and curriculum alignment to standards.
- Assess student understanding, and use the results to determine how to proceed.

As a leader, it is your responsibility to empower teachers by providing them with information and opportunities to grow. By sharing the strategies above with your staff, you will help transform mediocre teachers into exceptional teachers, and you will improve students' access to education by ensuring that each student is given the opportunity to learn from a quality educator.

Finding and Keeping Effective Teachers

By now you know that effective schools must have quality teachers, but how do you get them? Hiring, training, and retaining. Once you find quality teachers, you must take the time to find ways to make sure they stay at your school, or at least in the education field. Research shows that half of all teachers leave the profession within five years (Weber 2010). We can't expect students to receive a quality education if we can't keep effective educators in the profession. For both the school's efficiency and the students' achievement, it is important that schools learn to not only attract quality teachers but also retain them.

The best way to determine strategies that will be helpful to your school is reflecting on where you are and where you want to be. Before moving on to the tips and strategies in this section, take a few moments to complete the self-reflection exercise. Remember to be honest in your answers. Don't write down what you wish your school did; write down what your school is actually doing.

SELF-REFLECTION EXERCISE 6.1: REFLECTING ON SELECTING AND SUPPORTING AN EFFECTIVE STAFF

1) When do you begin recruiting and hiring staff for the next school year?

_____

_____

_____

_____

_____

2) How do you assess teacher qualifications?

_____

_____

_____

_____

_____

3) Describe your observation practices. Include when you observe, how often you observe, and what you record when you observe.

_____

_____

_____

_____

_____

4) When hiring, do you ask candidates what would make them leave if given the position?

_____

_____

_____

_____

_____

5) What questions do you frequently ask during the interview process?

_____

_____

_____

_____

_____

6) What categories do the professional development options you currently offer fall within (Relationships, Curriculum, and Pedagogy)? Are you addressing the weakest areas?

_____

_____

_____

_____

_____

7) What efforts do you make to retain quality teachers?

_____

_____

_____

_____

_____

8) What are the most common strengths and weaknesses among your teaching staff?

_____

_____

_____

_____

_____

9) How could you improve these weaknesses and use these strengths?

_____

_____

_____

_____

_____

10) How do you address ineffective teachers?

_____

_____

_____

_____

11) Besides developing your staff, how are you developing yourself professionally?

_____

_____

_____

_____

After completing the self-reflection exercise, you may have identified areas of improvement in this category. The following are simple recruitment and retention strategies to help you find and retain quality teachers.

- Recognize that recruiting is ongoing. You should start when the new year begins, and utilize your teaching staff to assist you with hiring, especially during December and May.
- Create a hiring pool, and hire early for content areas you know you will have annual openings for based on historical data.
- Conduct exit interviews. Use the data to strategize ways to improve hiring, staff development, and retaining policies.

- During recruitment interviews, ask candidates questions aimed at challenging situations that allows you to examine how effective they are at problem solving during tough circumstances. Also, ask questions that also measure their persistence. Effective teachers generally enjoy a challenge, and they do not easily give up.

- Ask teaching candidates, "What would make you leave if given the position?" This will help you determine if the candidate will be able to support your school's mission and related activities. In some interviews, teaching candidates have shared with me that home visits or late hours would cause them to leave because they have families that need their attention or they have fears about the community the school serves. Those candidates were not good matches for our school, and that one question helped reveal that, which saved the school time and money and allowed us to hire more suitable candidates.

- Collaborate with universities and learn from student teachers. For instance, you could conduct mock interviews or host a student teacher dinner and listen to what they share about your organization. Even if you are not recruiting at that time, student teachers will appreciate that you took the time to listen to them and you will likely learn new ways to improve.

- Reflect diversity in publications and on web pages. Attend hiring fairs at diverse university settings.

- Use a merit-based system to highlight outstanding teachers.

- Frequently assess teachers and give immediate feedback. In Montgomery County, we gave a carbonated walk-through sheet, which is in the appendix, when we walked through a teacher's classroom. Likewise, a carbonated central office walk-through form was used. This feedback gave the staff some immediate feedback.

- When conducting a formal observation, meet with the teacher or school leader within 48 hours. The closer to the event an individual gets feedback, the more impact the feedback will have. This is also true for student feedback, so encourage your staff to provide comments and suggestions quickly after assessing students.

- Provide resources and professional development opportunities that are aligned with the strategic goals and with building relationships. Collaboration time is essential. Teachers are the best staff developers for each other. It's important that programs and consultants for programs are not viewed as the only type of staff development.

- Change the evaluation language from punitive wording that describes needing improvement to language that addresses growth and development on a continuum of learning, and include data as part of that process. All teachers can grow, and the evaluation process should be one that supports teacher growth.

- Use current research, literature, and best practices from surrounding schools to engage teachers and instructional leaders in discussions on research and best practices.

- Provide competitive salaries and benefits. It's difficult for staff to be recruited when other organizations are not providing the support systems needed to provide the benefits you wish to offer. Competitive salaries are essential as we support staff in an increasingly difficult economy. It's interesting that the teaching profession is one of the lowest paid professional careers when every other career depends on the teaching professions to exist. Educators should be highly paid just as physicians and other professionals are. While schools may be unable to accomplish that task, they can be competitive with other school districts. The goal should be to demonstrate that fair and competitive compensation is a priority.

- Ask for input from all employees. For instance, you could hold open forums at staff meetings or create focus groups. Modeling this behavior will also have a positive impact on student achievement because it will illustrate an important strategy that teachers can use in their own classrooms.

- Introduce new teachers and students to the community through activities such as bus tours or weekend family events.
- Provide a resource room for teachers and parents. This will send an intentional message that you care about their growth and development.
- Focus on student learning and engagement when observing lessons. Look for student engagement, student performance, and evidence of implementation of a standards-based curriculum that encourages deep thinking. The depth of knowledge being asked for in assignments should be the focus of observations.

Incentives for Effective Teachers

Another way to attract and retain quality teachers is by implementing an incentive program. For instance, you may consider using incentive rewards to align achievement with salary scales in an effort to reward teachers for student achievement results. Most schools base salaries and promotions on factors such as seniority instead of student achievement. Research, however, shows that incentives based on student performance can motivate teachers to focus on student achievement and improve students' learning. Some schools simply do not allow teachers to progress on the salary scale unless there is evidence of high teacher performance.

Incentive programs often cause controversy because they differ greatly from the traditional education practices and because it's difficult to fairly apply such a model. One of the complications includes the fact that not all teachers have standardized student test scores as an outcome of their course.

Incentive programs are a new strategy that some school districts have experimented with, and research suggests that it is worth considering implementing an incentive program. When creating such a program, remember these key points:

- Don't reward and punish teachers for factors outside of their control. This includes factors such as socioeconomic status and family relationships. Not all students come to school equally prepared to learn. Therefore, consideration should be given to teachers growing in addition to meeting benchmarks. If you remember Maslow's Hierarchy of Needs, some students require basic needs before learning can begin. The goal is not to reward teachers for having students who already succeed. The goal is to encourage and reward teachers to improve achievement among all students, but especially among those who need the most help.

- Measure school performance accurately. While it is beneficial to look at group outcomes, it is also important to consider individual progress. If a teacher is able to increase academic gains among a handful of students, that is something worth praising.

- Don't rely solely on performance testing. These tests only show part of the picture. They don't account for all of the learning that takes place in a classroom, and they don't account for the contribution of the teacher to the school community.

Incentive programs can be effective if implemented properly. The strategies above are the foundation for a successful incentive program. If you are interested in implementing an incentive program, talk to leaders and teachers at schools who have experimented with this method. They will be able to provide honest feedback on what works and doesn't.

Hold Everyone Accountable

Every person working in a school system has the power to impact student achievement. All staff members, such as custodians and cafeteria workers, influence the school culture and climate. For instance, custodial staff must keep the school clean and safe, and they interact with students throughout the day. Likewise, cafeteria workers create relationships with students, which help develop a sense of community. Everyone who works for a school district can save a child's life by helping them succeed in school and teaching them valuable lessons such as discipline, respect, and responsibility. Therefore, it is important that schools hold all employees, regardless of title, accountable for student success rather than only focusing on the teaching staff.

Effective Leaders

In order for educators to implement strategies that will improve student achievement, they need support and guidance from effective leaders. Before reading the next set of tips for leaders, complete this self-reflection exercise.

SELF-REFLECTION 6.2: SCHOOL LEADERS

1) Name and describe at least two people you consider to be great leaders in your school district. They can be in any position ranging from cafeteria worker to superintendent.

_____

_____

_____

_____

_____

2) Name and describe two leaders you admire. They do not need to be educators. They can be relatives, politicians, entertainers, etc. List the leader on one side of the T chart and the characteristics they display in the second column.

Leader's Name	Admirable Characteristics
1.	
2.	

3) How would you define a great leader?

_____

_____

_____

_____

_____

4) Do you consider yourself an effective leader? Why or why not?

_____

_____

_____

_____

_____

Like teachers, leaders utilize many different leadership strategies to accomplish their goals. Despite the many variances in approaches and personalities, high performing school leaders often have several characteristics in common. Here are just a few of the many ways great leaders throughout history have been described. As you read through the list, reflect on how your school community describes you.

- They inspire others.
- They are innovative thinkers.
- People enthusiastically follow them, and they expend a great deal of effort aimed at improving their organization.
- They are skillful in building relationships and are diplomatic.
- They are lifelong learners and are always seeking ways to improve.
- They are open-minded and flexible.
- They are highly motivated and determined.
- They are positive thinkers and don't easily give up. Persistence and creativity in problem solving is evident.
- They are trustworthy and earn the respect of their followers.
- They have effective interpersonal skills.

- They are enthusiastic about their job and ideas. They are passionate about their work.
- They are confident.
- They remain calm under pressure. They don't let stress and obstacles disrupt them.
- They have a vision and continuously set goals.
- They have strong problem solving skills and know how to make decisions.
- They build teams aimed at continuous improvement.

These are just a few of the common characteristics of effective leaders. These characteristics can be observed in teachers and in principals as well as in leaders in any other profession. Take a moment to circle at least three characteristics above that you can improve to become a better leader. Now, jot down three steps you will take to improve those qualities in yourself.

Leadership Characteristic I will Develop	Action Steps to Improve
1.	
2.	
3.	

Now that you have identified the characteristics of great leaders in general, let's explore specific strategies for educational leaders.

- Be visible and demonstrate to your staff that you will only ask them to do things you are also willing to do yourself. I used this strategy by teaching in classrooms and serving lunches in the cafeteria while also serving as principal and as a superintendent. Putting myself in the shoes of my staff enabled me to see their perspective on matters, and it gave the teachers staff development and planning time by having a co-teacher. It also allowed me to build relationships with my staff and let me demonstrate that everyone in the school was a teacher. I wanted to show my staff that I understood their concerns and issues and that all of the work I did as an administrator was intended to support them and their students.

- Create mentorship programs for new teachers and school leaders. No teacher or school leader is perfect on the first day. In fact, I credit a large amount of my success to the mentors I've had throughout my career. It is essential that teachers and school leaders learn from each other, and it's critical that they have a colleague to go to with questions, concerns, and ideas.

- Hold all school employees responsible for student achievement. Teachers are not the only people who impact students' academic success. The actions and expectations of principals, policy makers, and administrators all effect student achievement. Students and staff should know the school's goals and mission, and they should know the overall school performance. I observed an effective principal at one school who demonstrated this as she took me on a tour of her school. As she passed random students she engaged them in discussions. These students could clearly articulate how many students were proficient and advanced, and they could share their school's goals. The full school community was held responsible for learning.

- Encourage teamwork among all school employees, not just teachers. If you want students to feel as though their school is a community, then the staff members must all act as a community.

- Provide teachers with the resources needed to do their jobs. Since money is always a concern, think of innovative ways to provide teachers with the resources they need. Resources include materials, time, and support. For instance, teachers need collaboration time and support to effectively do their job. When I became a principal in St. Louis City, one of the first things I did was create a supply room that granted teachers access to paper, pencils, etc. The teachers were ecstatic. It was as if I had given them a pay raise. Given the amount of money most teachers spend on student supplies, perhaps it was like giving them a pay increase. It's essential that leaders remove the obstacles that hinder the delivery of effective instruction. Surprisingly, it's fairly common that school systems limit the instructional materials teachers and school leaders are granted, which teachers and school leaders need to properly support their students and staff. Providing adequate supplies is one immediate area that school leaders should address in their budgets that will lead to an improved culture. Teachers will immediately notice and appreciate the support, and it's a step that sends an instant message to students and parents. In one district were I served as superintendent, the district provided all families with school supplies. That year, achievement and parental involvement significantly increased. Parents felt we were genuinely concerned about ensuring that students had the tools they needed to achieve at high levels, so the parents became more involved in supporting the school. That one action was a relationship builder, and it had a ripple effect that helped us improve attendance because a lack of supplies was no longer an excuse.
- Provide teachers with the time to create lessons, review performance, and improve skills. By helping teachers become better educators, you are increasing the likelihood of consistently high academic achievement that is sustainable.

- Manage finances responsibly. Budgets are always a major concern for most school districts, so relieve some of this stress by making smart financial decisions that keep student achievement a priority.
- Define a vision for the school, and make sure all of your actions reflect that vision. Also, make sure teachers, parents, and students are aware of your vision through your actions, your web page, and the messages shared through school publications.
- Serve as a mentor and role model.
- Acknowledge your staff's hard work and talents. For instance, you could host an award dinner or celebrate an outstanding teacher.
- Show teachers that you value their time. For instance, don't waste time in lengthy meetings when a short memo would suffice. As a principal, chief academic officer, and superintendent, a strategy I used to ensure meetings were focused on staff development instead of operational matters included sending out a weekly instructional update to staff members. The update included information from departments who wanted to share information. This freed up time and allowed us to document the information we sent to schools. An example of this document is located in the appendix.
- Provide staff members with support systems to address professional and personal needs.
- Inspire others by sharing success stories about schools with similar demographics and be prepared to learn from others.
- Be visible, available, and have the courage to take the necessary steps, which may be unpopular at times, to hold everyone accountable for high achievement.

Create a Plan for Improvement

Now that you have a variety of strategies to improve instructional leadership in your school and classrooms, take a few minutes to consider how you will use this information to improve student achievement. Go back through this chapter and circle or highlight all of the strategies you'd like to implement and characteristics you'd like to adopt. Then, create an action plan. What steps will you take to implement these strategies or characteristics? When will you enact these strategies? How will you measure your success? Who will you hold accountable for specific tasks? Remember, one of the qualities of effective instructional leaders is planning ahead.

To ensure that you address all of the questions above, I encourage you to use the SMART goals template. An example of a SMART Goal template is shown below to help you get started. For a detailed example of an action plan, turn to the sample located in the appendix.

Note that the goal should be measurable and specific, and the items listed as activities are numbered. For the purpose of this example, only one activity is listed; however, based on the goal, more activities may be required. Placing your goals in a SMART goal template will help you hold yourself and others accountable in a visible manner by encouraging you and your staff to meet specific benchmarks. To start creating transformational change, you need to create a plan and start working towards your goals.

Table 6.1: SMART Goals

Goal: An aligned, standards-based curriculum that ensures instruction is paced to allow 100% of the state assessed content material to be taught.

Specific Activity	Measurement (What will be the evidence of completion?)	Assignable/ Achievable (Who will be assigned the action/activity?)	Realistic Resources (What budget or other resources will you use to address the activity?)	Timeline (When will the activity occur and be complete?)	Professional Development
Activity #1of 2 Develop a curriculum scope and sequence	Completed scope and sequence curriculum documents	Curriculum Coordinators, Director of Curriculum	Teachers, Training Stipends, Model curriculum, State assessment goal	July 1, 2013	Train staff in curriculum writing format

Now, use the blank chart below to begin creating your plan. You may want to copy the page so you can complete the chart for multiple goals.

Goal:

Specific Activity	Measurement (What will be the evidence of completion?)	Assignable/ Achievable (Who will be assigned the action/activity?)	Realistic Resources (What budget or other resources will you use to address the activity?)	Timeline (When will the activity occur and be complete?)	Professional Development
Activity # _ of _					

CHAPTER 7

It's Not Just How You Teach, It's What You Teach

"The more you read, the more things you will know. The more that you learn, the more places you'll go."

- Dr. Seuss

SO FAR, WE have discussed the characteristics of effective teachers and leaders, tips for building relationships and cultures, and the problems in American public schools. We've covered how quality teachers help students learn, but we haven't talked about the curriculum those teachers use. A high achieving school must focus on the three areas of the tripod: relationships, pedagogy, and curriculum. One without the other will not produce the highest possible results. Before we delve into the type of curriculum used by effective schools, let's take a moment to reflect on your school's current curriculum.

SELF–REFLECTION 7.1: YOUR SCHOOL'S CURRICULUM

1) Do you have an aligned, standards-based curriculum with literacy integrated in all content areas in place that is uniform K-12?

_____

_____

_____

_____

_____

2) Is the curriculum easy to understand and follow?

_____

_____

_____

_____

_____

3) Has there been adequate staff development in curriculum?

_____

_____

_____

_____

_____

4) Was the curriculum written for teachers or by teachers?

_____

_____

_____

_____

_____

If you do not have a strong curriculum in place, begin curriculum writing in reading and math, then integrate those subjects in all other areas (including PE, art, and music). Research shows that effective schools spend more time on communication arts and mathematics than poorer performing schools. These two subjects are the foundation for all other subjects, and they are the most commonly used outside of the classroom. If the ancillary courses had a curriculum in place that mirrored the standards for math and reading along with their course standards, imagine how fast students would progress in math and reading. In one of the highest performing schools in Montgomery County, where I led as superintendent, the art teacher had art lessons and standards posted that showed the complete integration of math and literacy in her curriculum. Students would leave her class learning art while also learning literacy and math standards.

Math and reading are the two areas where the achievement gap is most evident. For example, take a look at this chart adapted from a 2009 McKensey and Company report that shows the gap between middle class Caucasian white students and African American students in the area of fourth grade math. This chart shows that by fourth grade, middle class white students in the highest performing states are approximately five years ahead of middle class black students in the poor performing district of Washington, DC.

Table 7.1: NAEP Grade 4 Math Scores in Public Schools 2007

Group of Students	NAEP Score
Middle class whites in NJ (top state for the group)	257
Low income whites (average)	236
Middle class blacks (average)	232
Low income blacks in DC (bottom region for group)	206

This chart is adapted from information in the 2009 McKensey and Company report "The Economic Impact of the Achievement Gap in America's Schools." Averages were determined for groups based on income. Low income is defined by free or reduced lunch eligibility.

Using the techniques outlined in this book school leaders I have had the privilege to serve with and lead, have significantly improved math and reading scores in their schools. Some of the transformations are shown below at Shawsville Elementary School and Blacksburg High School in Montgomery County. They represent two high performing schools on opposite ends of the same school district with different demographic groups. However, both remained committed to eliminating achievement gaps. Those two are examples of what many others have accomplished in their own schools. Below are a few examples of how we used data to monitor the students' improvement in math and reading. (We will look more closely at how to use data in an upcoming chapter.)

Table 7.2: Shawsville Elementary School
Gap Analysis for Disadvantaged Students (Math)
2003-2007

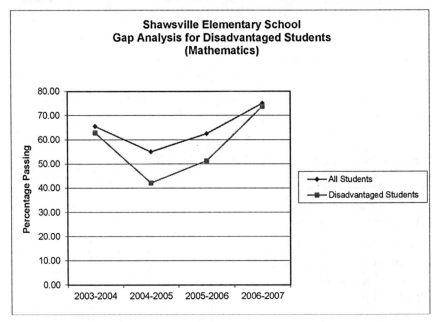

Table 7.3: Shawsville Elementary School
Gap Analysis for Disadvantaged Students (Reading)
2003-2007

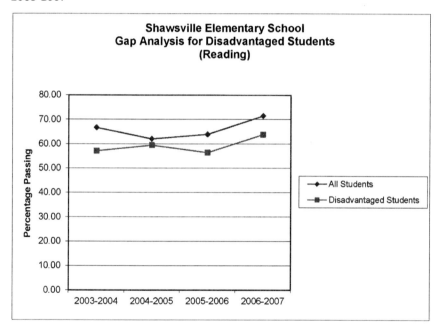

Table 7.4: Blacksburg High School
Gap Analysis for Limited English Proficient Students (Reading)
2003-2007

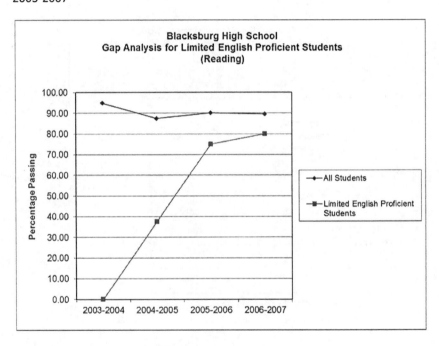

Table 7.5: Blacksburg High School
Gap Analysis for African American Students (Reading)
2003-2007

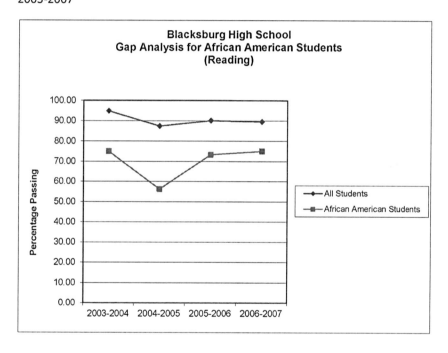

Integrate Literacy in Every Class

Effective schools recognize that reading needs to take place in every classroom regardless of the subject, and teachers need to expose children to quality reading materials. This will not only make the students better readers, but it will also make them more knowledgeable on the subjects being taught. For instance, a history teacher can enrich a lesson by having students read primary and secondary sources in addition to the textbook. These extra materials will expand the students' knowledge of the subject, make the lesson more interesting and valuable, provide an accurate and balanced historical perspective, and help the students become better readers.

If you're thinking that the students already receive enough reading time in their language arts courses, consider this revelation. An investigation of New York City Public Schools revealed that students spent an average of 10 minutes a day reading in school, and 40% of those students did no reading at all (Lemov 2010). How can students learn to read and excel on state tests if they have such limited time devoted reading? They can't.

Think about your own school schedule and the percentage of time devoted to literacy compared to the amount of hours in a day. On average, in a seven hour school day, three hours are left for instruction after specialty classes, breakfast, lunch, restroom breaks, recess, passing periods, and possibly other non-instructional events such as assemblies that may occur. If literacy is not integrated in every subject matter skillfully, students will not be exposed to enough literacy-based lessons and their improvements in this area will be limited.

This is not just a problem in New York City. It is estimated that in most schools, students spend less than one hour per day reading. This is a huge problem because reading is essential to students' success. The best way to increase student reading time is by including it in other classes besides language arts and English. In fact, the popular education book *Teach Like a Champion* suggests that "the overall value of the additional high-quality reading you could do in a typical school day could equal or possibly exceed the value of what happens in designated reading classes"(Lemov 2010). Based on Lemov's assertion, we can conclude that schools need to make every effort to include more reading throughout the school day.

But it's not just the amount of time that students spend reading, it is also the material and way they read. By incorporating reading in other subject areas, we can teach students important skills that are relevant to real life. In a standard high school English class, students will read a novel or other piece of literature and analyze the text for meaning and identify important elements such as themes, characters, etc. While this is a great skill to have, an equal amount of time must involve engaging students in high level comprehension, vocabulary, and problem solving lessons that cause students to relate literature to their lives.

Pretend you want to start a garden. You heard a report on the news about the health benefits of eating more fresh produce, and a neighbor recently told you that growing your own vegetables is more environmentally friendly than purchasing them at the grocery store. You've always wanted to reduce your carbon footprint so your grandchildren have a beautiful earth to enjoy, and your doctor recently told you that you need to start eating healthier. Starting a garden sounds like a perfect idea, but there is only one problem: You don't know the first thing about gardening. So what do you do?

Most likely, you go to the bookstore or library and find some books on gardening. While you're there, you might also pick up a few magazines on the subject. Later that night, while checking your email, you search the web and print out a few articles about growing vegetables. That weekend, you spend your time reading all the materials, following the directions, and starting a garden. You spend all summer tending to your garden, and whenever you have a problem, such as pesky bugs, you return to your books and find a solution. By the end of the summer, you have a garden full of fresh produce and you feel accomplished and capable of tackling the project again next year. So what happened here? You used a variety of texts to solve a problem, which is the same skill students need to learn in school.

Utilizing a variety of texts is important for developing readers.

In addition, students need to learn how to decode, inference, and comprehend. These are skills that can be taught in any class, and they will serve students well as they continue their education and become working adults. In addition, you will improve students' writing because students who read well tend to write well. This is important because poor writing can negatively impact academic performance. To improve students' reading and writing in your school, implement these strategies:

- Encourage all teachers to increase time spent on reading in engaging ways, and have them frequently assess students' reading ability by asking comprehension questions and having students read aloud.
- Have teachers use developmentally appropriate quality literature and novel sets in every grade level. District level administrators should commit resources to purchasing leveled readers and novels for every school to ensure equitable resources.
- In one high performing elementary school I visited, the principal required students to always have a book in their hands when they walked through the halls. This ensured that students always had something with them to read and allowed students to use downtime productively. The message the principal gave students regarding the important of literacy was powerful.
- Urge teachers to use a variety of texts, including fiction and nonfiction books, magazines, and newspapers. They should also include primary and secondary sources. All of these texts have value by connecting students to the broader society and to current events.
- Request that every teacher, regardless of the subject, include vocabulary within lessons that align with standards and the standardized assessments. High performing classes are clearly focused on literacy regardless of what content area being taught. All classrooms, including art, music, and PE, in K-12 settings can have a print-rich classroom and a word wall. Imagine

how much a student would learn and remember if they saw the same vocabulary and definitions in multiple classrooms.

- Encourage all teachers to include a variety of writing assignments. These should include short response answers on tests or homework as well as longer documents such as research papers.
- Ensure that teachers use specialized instruction to accommodate various interests and skill levels.
- Make books and other reading materials easily accessible for students, parents, and teachers. Some schools limit the ability to check out materials or use textbooks at home, while expecting students to study and read outside of school. The replacement costs of materials must be included within any realistic school budget; it is essential that schools allow students access to reading materials. One of the first purchases I generally make in schools I lead is classroom libraries, which are refreshed annually.
- Educate all teachers on how to teach important skills such as decoding, fluency, inferences, and comprehension.
- Have teachers use short durations of reading to encourage concentration.

Improving Math Scores

Like reading, every teacher can find ways to incorporate math into their subject. For instance, in history class, students can figure out the time that has passed between major events by subtracting dates. In English, students can use probability to determine the likelihood of an outcome, and in science, students can use math in a variety of ways such as measuring liquids. Here are a few simple tips for improving students' achievement in math:

- Have high expectations. Math is a teachable skill, and every student is capable of succeeding in this subject. Being good in math is not something you are; it's something you attain.

Every student should be empowered with knowing they can improve in this area.

- Increase students' confidence. How often have you heard someone say "I'm just not a math person"? There is no such thing as a "math person." Make students and teachers believe that they can succeed in this subject despite previous struggles. Teachers who feel they are inadequate in teaching math (which is common among many elementary teachers because they focus on general education courses) relay these sentiments to students.

- Ensure rigor and higher level activities are within the curriculum. Show students and teachers that you believe in them by helping them reflect and reach the outlined targeted goals, which should be at or above the grade level they are in.

- Provide a structured support system that offers extra help outside of the regular school day to students who need.

- Train math teachers to remove the psychological barriers associated with the subject and train staff to differentiate instruction while still challenging students.

- After taking several teachers on a visit to the Ron Clark Academy, a high performing school in Atlanta, several teachers returned and began incorporating music and movement in their math lessons. Elementary and secondary students alike were having fun learning math as they incorporated dance moves and songs to mathematic formulas. As students became more engaged, learning increased. Support teachers in finding ways to make learning fun.

Aligning Curriculum with State Standards

High performing schools realize that educators' and students' success is often based on standardized test scores, but they balance those lessons with other essential skills that will not be on standardized tests such as social skills and character traits. I believe that by addressing the whole child, schools create better problem solvers and genuine lifelong learners who are better students in all academic areas. It is important for educators to emphasize the standards and expectations on the state tests while also addressing other subjects and skills that will benefit the students. If educators simply teach to the test, students will be robbed of important lessons that will benefit them both in school and in the real world. Remember students should be learning standards that the state assessments are aligned with in addition to preparing for the assessment format.

While there is controversy surrounding the effectiveness of standardized tests and the feedback they provide, it does not appear as though these standards will be going away any time soon. In fact, research shows that there are benefits to these standards. According Eric Jensen's book *Teaching with Poverty in Mind*, standards have the following positive results:

- Standardized assessments expose racial and socioeconomic disparities because schools must report the results for demographic subgroups. This allows educators to identify which standards and strategies to focus on in order to close the gaps.
- Standardized assessments provide disadvantaged students with other educational opportunities because schools that don't achieve AYP must provide students with the option to transfer or receive additional services. As a result, schools must ensure that every classroom has a qualified teacher and that they are providing the best education possible.
- Standardized assessments promote focusing on results and an aligned curriculum.
- Standardized assessments ensure that instructional targets are set at the same level regardless of the school.

Based on these benefits, it is essential that educators adapt their curriculum and instruction to improve how teachers apply standards and focus on alignment and quality instruction. Some practical steps you can use to begin aligning your school's curriculum with state standards and improving students' test scores are listed below.

- Educate teachers on state standards and best practices.
- Implement data-driven practices. Most universities do not provide courses on utilizing data to improve instruction. Therefore, leaders must develop teachers in this area to ensure they are strategic with improving instruction and with writing curriculum to address standards effectively.
- Implement quarterly benchmark assessments and develop weekly common assessments that are implemented across grade levels and are aligned with the standards and curriculum. Promote vertical team planning to enable staff to review performance across grade levels. Principals can promote collaborative planning by adding time at the beginning of each staff meeting or by creating common planning times in the master schedule. As a principal and superintendent, I did both to ensure teachers had enough time to plan thoughtfully.
- Visit high performing schools to observe their instructional methods and find ways to make improvements in your school.
- Encourage teachers to consider individual student needs when creating lessons and adapting teaching methods. For instance, research shows that boys and girls have different educational needs. According to an article published in *Educational Leadership*, an Association for Supervision and Curriculum Development publication, girls' brains are hardwired to have "more sensually detailed memory storage, better listening skills, and better discrimination among the various tones of voice" (Gurian and Stevens 2004). This explains why female students tend to outperform male students in the areas of reading and writing. The article also states that boys are more likely to be physically impulsive, have shorter attention spans, and are less capable of multi-tasking. These key differences should be considered when instructing students. Some

districts are currently experimenting with gender-specific schools and courses. Keep an eye on these trends to learn about new findings.

- Write and implement a well-paced curriculum document that aligns with state standards. In this document, the standards should be listed first, followed by activities, pacing, assessment, and resources.

- Advise teachers to include various sources and cultures to provide an accurate, balanced historical perspective. As a superintendent, I have always included social justice training as part of the staff development for teachers to promote culturally relevant teaching behaviors.

- Pace the standards into daily objectives. These should be measurable and manageable. Schools should refine the curriculum in this fashion, and teachers should pace their instruction accordingly.

- Make objectives and learning targets visible, and remain focused on the target.

- Review the standards and group concepts and skills that go together. Group these items together to create units.

- Suggest that teachers create themes for each unit and use essential questions to relate to those themes. These questions should be open-ended and general to encourage deep levels of thinking. One middle school in Montgomery County, a district I led as superintendent, used a thematic approach to courses of study and lesson plans. The model was called "Content Enhancement," which heightened learning through thematic units. Scores increased as a result of this method.

- Update content, methods, and assessments to make information more relevant to today's society. We should be preparing students for the future rather than just teaching the same materials that have always been taught. Make sure textbooks are current. Use technology as much as possible, and use new forms of assessment such as WebQuests. This requires you and your staff members to be lifelong learners.

- Don't forget about the arts. These subjects are often the first to go when budgets get tight, but they are essential to developing students as a whole. We need to encourage creativity and self-expression. These are the skills that make people innovators and leaders.

- When creating lesson plans, teachers should consider the sequence and pace. Principals should expect teachers to turn in lesson plans, preferably in a simple online format. This allows principals to have an annual look at how instruction was paced compared to year-end results. It also serves as another accountability measure to ensure a plan is in place each day in every classroom.

- Advise teachers to always gain benchmark data through pre- and post-test scores to assess students' knowledge before and after the lesson. They should also assess students' learning daily to adjust lesson plans before moving on to new material. Mastery for all students is key, and teachers must have the ability to differentiate lessons within a group to accomplish this. In one district, I realigned the budget and hired certified teaching assistants to support the small group instruction I expected for mastery learning.

- Integrate media literacy. Social media and technology are changing the way we live, interact, and get information. If we are trying to prepare students to be successful in the real world, then we need to teach them these essential skills. Encourage teachers to look for ways to incorporate music, videos, social media sites, blogs, podcasts, and virtual forums when creating lessons and activities. Not only will these lessons teach students valuable skills, but they will also engage the learner because they are relatable and trendy.

- Consider double blocking math and reading courses in ways that increase engagement. It's not effective to have ineffective instructors with poor engagement to have students with them for longer periods. It is effective, however, to allow some students to have extended time to become fully engaged and process material within the extended time. This takes a great deal of personalization in matching a student's schedule based on their needs and ensuring teaching styles are considered when placing students in classes.

- Encourage teachers to observe each other teaching. When observing, know why teachers are teaching a particular lesson. What will the students learn? Why should they know this information?

Reflect on the information in this chapter and begin making plans for improvement in your school. In the chart below, jot down three ways you will increase time in teaching reading and math to improve student achievement.

Self-Refection 7.2: Improving Math and Reading

Math	Reading
1.	1.
2.	2.
3.	3.

CHAPTER **8**

Don't Forget About Assessment

"Any genuine teaching will result, if successful, in someone's knowing how to bring about a better condition of things than existed earlier."

- - John Dewey

YOU MAY HAVE noticed that the concept of monitoring and assessment has repeatedly been mentioned throughout this book. In each section, there are tips on monitoring and assessing the success of your school within the three areas of the tripod: relationships, pedagogy, and curriculum. That is because all effective schools understand that every successful education system needs to frequently and continuously monitor their students, staff, programs, and methods. Without this, improvement becomes stagnant.

Think about an exercise and diet program. You make a New Year's resolution to lose weight and get healthy, so you make some small changes to your diet to reduce calories and start walking thirty minutes a day. To monitor the results, you weigh yourself twice weekly. For the first two months, you lose an average of a pound a week. Then, you suddenly hit a plateau. You're still walking thirty minutes a day, and you are still limiting your calorie intake. You don't know why you can't lose any more weight, so you assume you must be cursed with a poor metabolism and you give up. If you'd done things just a little differently, you could have broken through that plateau and achieved the results you wanted. All you needed was to thoroughly monitor and assess your efforts, progress, and results.

If you had assessed your diet, you would have realized that while you were limiting your calories, you were still consuming a large amount of junk food that contained empty calories. By including more nutrient-dense foods in your diet, you would have helped your body more efficiently burn calories and thus, lost more weight. In addition, if you'd assessed your exercise routine, you would have noticed that your body had become accustomed to your thirty minute walk and was no longer challenged. You would have also realized that you were missing strength training, which increases lean muscle mass and revs up your metabolism. By changing your routine to meet these new areas of weakness, you could have dramatically improved your results. Instead, you tried a few strategies and quit after achieving only minimum results. The same scenario happens every day in schools across the country.

Administrators or teachers will attend an inspiring conference or read a motivating book and decide to implement changes to improve their students' academic achievement. After spending a few months using the strategies they learned, the improvement reaches a plateau. The educators become frustrated and decide that their struggling students will never reach the same levels as their peers, so they stop trying to increase improvement. They just quit. As a result, the students suffer because they don't have educators who persist in helping them improve. When the test results come out, the achievement gap is still there.

According to Victoria L. Bernhardt, PhD (2004), most schools only fully implement a plan for the first six to twelve months after the plan is complete. This does not have to be the case in your school. There is a simple solution to this detrimental problem that so many educators experience. All you have to do is frequently monitor and assess your students, staff, self, programs, and strategies. By doing so, you will identify areas that need improvement, and you can adjust your action plan and strategies to overcome those obstacles. Closing the achievement gap is not easy, but it is possible. Just think about all the schools that have created the transformational change you want to initiate in your school, and remember that if they can do it, you can do it.

Effective schools and educators know that monitoring achievement and assessing various areas of the school will help improve student outcomes. Here are some tips for monitoring and assessing success in your school.

- Routinely gather staff members to discuss and assess programs and strategies. Determine what is working, what needs improvement, and what is not working at all. Then brainstorm strategies to turn those strengths and weaknesses into a plan for improvement. School improvement should be ongoing and data driven.
- Use a variety of tools such as walk-through observations, formal observations, benchmark assessments, student portfolios, and teachers' conversations to monitor the successful implementation of best practices.
- Schedule regular classroom visits, and frequently hold conferences with teachers, students, and parents.
- Recognize and celebrate what is working.
- Encourage departments and teams to meet regularly to assess student progress and brainstorm solutions to obstacles.
- Ask for student, staff, and parent feedback to assess elements such as school culture and support services. Also, encourage all staff members to share their suggestions and opinions. Using this feedback to monitor school progress and programs and to implement new practices demonstrates that you value the input of the school community.
- Think of assessment as a physician treating a patient. The doctor must assess the ailment to determine the appropriate treatment. Then, he or she will monitor the patient's progress and adjust treatment as needed. Educators must use the same process to improve student achievement. First, identify the problem. Then, create a plan to address the problem. Once

the plan has been implemented, periodically monitor improvement and adjust your approach accordingly.

- Make sure staff is utilizing data teams by making date consultation a common routine. Individuals are hardwired to think in patterns and repeat habits. By creating positive routines and patterns, you can create positive results. For instance, if you make assessment and data review teams a routine practice, students and staff will begin to automatically assess themselves and others and use data to improve strategies. Therefore, you will create a positive pattern that leads to academic improvement.

- When observing classrooms, focus on the depth of knowledge (DOK) rather than the amount of work being accomplished. Also, look at the quality and frequency of student assessments. Teachers will focus on the areas you assess, so be sure to measure what matters most. Therefore, by assessing DOK in lessons and the assessments used, you are encouraging teachers to focus on DOK and assessment techniques that will ultimately improve student achievement.

- In post observation conferences, ask teachers to list three pieces of evidence that prove students have mastered the concept and to describe the strategies being implemented to reinforce students' understanding.

- While observing classrooms, draw a chart of the room, number the students, and note student engagement. This will help you initiate a discussion on student engagement during the post observation conference.

- Require staff members to evaluate themselves. This forces teachers to reflect on their practices and achievements and promotes personal growth.

- Consider using peer evaluations. These provide another perspective on which to base assessment.

- Provide feedback as soon as possible. The closer to evaluation teachers receive feedback, the more impact the comments will have. This is also true for student evaluations, so encourage teachers to provide feedback to students as soon as possible after assessment.

Using Data

Effective schools understand the importance of researching and using data. This includes data on best practices and new theories as well as data on your schools' progress, demographics, student learning, and perceptions. This information provides facts on which to base decisions. Rather than simply adopting the newest practices in education, effective schools use data to understand how it will serve the students' needs and the impact the practices will have. In addition, data helps educators identify the root cause of a problem rather than just the symptoms.

Think about a doctor's visit. You've been having stomach problems for several weeks now. At first, you try several over-the-counter remedies to ease your symptoms. Some provide a little relief, but it is obvious that the problem is still there. So you finally decide to go to the doctor to find out what is causing the trouble. He does several tests and asks you a list of questions. By the time you're done, you find out that you are allergic to gluten and need to adjust your diet. Once you do, your stomach feels much better and you no longer need the over-the-counter medications.

Schools need to approach problems in the same manner as a doctor would. Treating the symptoms will only result in minimum improvement, and after a while, it may stop working. To create long-term, transformational change, you need to use data to fully assess performance and determine the root cause of the problem. Once you do this, you must continuously monitor the situation to determine the effectiveness of your solution and adjust accordingly.

In addition to helping you identify the root cause, data analysis helps you identify areas that need improvement, create a plan for improvement, provide feedback on performance, assess your progress, and determine if programs are working. It is important to look at four key areas when analyzing data: school progress, demographics, student learning, and perceptions (Bernhardt 2004). One of the best ways to do this is to use a data warehouse that allows you to analyze data across all four categories. This helps you disaggregate and intersect data in many ways and allows you to easily build graphs and create reports. There are many types of systems and software available.

Remember, data is to be used to inform and educate in order to improve instruction and student achievement. Data is not to be used to punish and penalize. In fact, using data to punish students or staff causes them to retreat to using excuses for academic failure, and teachers and students avoid looking at data if it's used in this manner. Instead, use data as a way to encourage growth and improvement.

Effective educators realize that data is all around them. Just a few examples include standardized student achievement data, predictive and formative assessment data, student grades, writing samples and rubrics, student and staff attendance, and discipline data. Although the information is readily available, we must have the courage to examine our own data, compare ourselves, and set goals of where we want to be. We must also seek to be transparent in sharing our data with our school community by displaying it on bulletin boards, banners, web pages, and in data rooms.

Examine the data by looking at:

- District wide achievement scores.
- Overall scores by content area for three to five years. Compare these numbers to predictive assessment data to identify the accuracy of predictive tests. This will help you effectively predict outcomes.
- School data by subgroup, student, teacher, content area, and grade level.
- Trend data to show improvements in attendance, discipline, and achievement.
- Comparative data between the district, schools, classrooms, grade levels, content areas, and national benchmarks.

- Accreditation and benchmark data by the number of students that need to improve annually.
- Data by student name and photo to further personalize who is behind the number.
- Data maps for staff and principals based on assessments and observations of behaviors.

Now, take a few minutes to reflect on your current methods for monitoring and assessing student and staff achievement. This will help you determine where you need to focus your improvement efforts. Short reflections like the ones used throughout this book are a tool for you to think about what you are doing, why, and how to improve your own practices. Periodically, take some time to reflect on what you're doing or not doing, what you hope to achieve, and how you can accomplish your goals. These exercises highlight your areas of weakness and strength, and they provide the foundation for plans that can create transformational change in your school.

SELF-REFLECTION 8.1: MONITORING AND ASSESSMENT PRACTICES

1) How do you know if your students are achieving at high levels? How do you identify areas that need improvement?

_____

_____

_____

_____

_____

2) What are ways you can use data to compare trend data relative to other grade levels across the school?

_____

_____

_____

_____

_____

3) How do you know your students will perform at high levels on the year-end assessments?

_____

_____

_____

_____

_____

4) How would you describe your monitoring and assessment routines?

_____

_____

_____

_____

_____

Now that you have an understanding of your current assessment efforts, revisit the list of tips for improving your monitoring and assessment techniques. Choose at least three strategies you plan to implement and write action steps for each goal. Use the chart below to complete this exercise.

Monitoring and Assessment Goal	Action Steps
1.	
2.	
3.	

CHAPTER 9

Final Words and Resources

"Success will not lower its standard to us. We must raise our standard to success."

- - Rev. Randall R. McBride, Jr.

I HOPE THIS book has shown you that high achievement is possible in all schools and that it has provided you with the tools you need to create transformational change. This book is just the beginning of your journey. Improvement takes time but should occur within the first year. Students do not have years to wait on our ability to improve. There will be ups and downs, and there may be moments you will want to give up. But always remember, that nothing is impossible and that every child is capable of succeeding. With consistency in implementing researched-based, effective strategies coupled with faith and determination, you can change the world by transforming the quality of schools.

Creating transformational change requires you to continuously learn and improve. This book provides you with the foundation for success. It is a resource, and like all resources, you must use it strategically and personalize the strategies to create an individual approach. It is up to you to implement the strategies that will have the greatest impact on your school. Continue monitoring and assessing your data to refine your goals and to develop effective strategies targeting those goals. Ron Edmonds once shared, "We can, whenever we choose, successfully teach children whose schooling is of interest to us. We already know more than we need to do that. Whether or not we do it must finally depend on how we feel about the fact we haven't so far." Studying other schools across the nation that are improving empowers us to see what's possible and begin creating change in our communities.

During this journey of continuous improvement, you must continue to seek out best practices. Therefore, I have provided a list of additional resources that will help you transform your school and show others what's truly possible for students. Below you will find a list of suggested books, articles, and websites that offer data, strategies, and inspirational stories. Following this chapter, you will also find an appendix that includes various documents that will be beneficial to your transformational work. These documents will help you implement some of the strategies discussed throughout this book. For privacy purposes, all personal information, such as school names, has been changed. These documents are meant to serve as templates for you to revise as needed as you implement the strategies in this book.

Continue to improve, continue to courageously set high expectations and expect more than what was produced in the past. Most importantly, continue to serve! Thank you for being an educational leader who seeks to transform environments into places where children thrive and exceed what's expected. Educators shape the future generation, and it is our job to provide them with the best future possible. Every child deserves to succeed, and every child is capable of performing at high levels if they are properly supported. I encourage you to lead in ways that inspire, energize, and cause others to dream big and reflect on how they can improve the quality of schools for all children.

Suggested Readings

"A Simple Justice" by W. Ayers and M. Klonsky

Closing the Achievement Gap: A Vision for Changing Beliefs and Practices by Belinda Williams

Closing the Achievement Gap: No Excuses by Patricia Davenport and Gerald Anderson

Closing the Achievement Gap: Reaching and Teaching Poverty Learners: 101 Top Strategies to Help High Poverty Learners Succeed by Tiffany Chane'l Anderson

Creating the Opportunity to Learn: Moving from Research to Practice to Close the Achievement Gap by A. Wade Boykin and Pedro Noguero

Curriculum 21: Essential Education for a Changing World by Heidi Hayes Jacobs

Data Analysis for Continuous School Improvement by Victoria L. Bernhardt, Ph.D

"Dispelling the Myth: Lessons from High-performing Schools" by Education Trust

Driven by Data: A Practical Guide to Improve Instruction by Paul Bambrick-Santoyo

Leading Change in Your School: How to Conquer Myths, Build Commitment, and Get Results by Douglas B. Reeves

Leading for Instructional Improvement: How Successful Leaders Develop Teaching and Learning Expertise by Stephen Fink and Anneke Markholt

Professional Capital: Transforming Teaching in Every School by Andy Hargreaves and Michael Fullan

"Rethinking Accountability: Voices in Urban Education" by Annenberg Foundation

Revising Professional Learning Communities at Work: New Insights

for Improving Schools by Richard DuFour, Rebecca DuFour, and Robert Eaker

Taking Charge: Leading with Passion and Purpose in the Principalship by Paul L. Shaw

Teach Like a Champion: 49 Techniques That Put Students On The Path To College by Doug Lemov

Teaching With Poverty In Mind: What Being Poor Does to Kids' Brains and What Schools Can Do About It by Eric Jensen

The Dream Keepers: Successful Teachers of African American Children by Gloria Ladson-Billings

"Transforming the American High School" by M. Cohen

"Trust in Schools: A core Resource for Improvement" by A. S. Bryk and B. L. Schneider

Waiting for "SUPERMAN" by Karl Weber

Finding Your Leadership Focus: What Matters Most For Student Results by Douglas B. Reeves

Whatever It Takes: How Professional Learning Communities Respond When Kids Don't Learn by Richard DuFour, Rebecca DuFour, Robert Eaker, and Gayle Karhanek

Young, Gifted, and Black: Promoting High Achievement Among African American Students by Theresa Perry, Claude Steele, and Asa Hillard III

Suggested Websites

The Education Trust
http://www.edtrust.org/

NYU Steinhardt School of Culture, Education, and Human
Development
http://steinhardt.nyu.edu/

The Tripod Project
http://tripodproject.org/

Change Leaders
http://www.changeleaders.info/

Marva Collins
http://www.marvacollins.com/biography.html

State of California Department of Education
http://www.closingtheachievementgap.org/cs/ctag/print/htdocs/
home.htm

Appendix

THE FOLLOWING PAGES contain templates for documents discussed in this book as well as other information you may find useful as you strive to create transformational change in your school. For privacy purposes, all school names and other personal information has been changed.

Mission Statement

The mission statement for XYZ School is to ensure all students achieve at high levels by eliminating achievement gaps and graduating well-prepared, college-ready students who succeed in their chosen careers and postsecondary schools.

Vision Statement

The vision of XYZ School is to nurture each child and shape futures as we develop lifelong learners. The XYZ School works as a team for continuous improvement. The XYZ School believes in fostering strong college and community partnerships that prepare students to become lifelong learners and productive citizens who contribute in positive ways to society.

Guiding Principles/Code of Ethics

We believe that collectively, we can ensure all students achieve at high levels. Therefore, we will continuously reflect on our own performance, engage in courageous conversations that hold ourselves and others accountable, and constantly seek ways to improve our own performance and the performance of our students. In classrooms in our school, you should see the following behaviors...

To develop a good answer,
remember the RASP strategy.

R

RESTATE THE QUESTION

A

ANSWER ALL OF THE PARTS

S

SUPPORT FROM THE TEXT

P

PERSONAL CONNECTION, OPINION,
EXTENSION

SAMPLE PRINCIPAL WALK-THROUGH
ELEMENTARY RECORD FORM

Teacher: _____ Date: _____

Activity(s) Observed:

Planning	*Observed	_Instruction_	*Observed
1. Written plans accurately describe:		1. Instruction is highly correlated to written plans.	_____
a. Lesson objective(s).	_____	2. Instruction ensures that students are actively engaged by:	
b. Lesson activities.	_____	a. Completing class work.	_____
c. Lesson assessment.	_____	b. Participating in discussions.	_____
2. Necessary materials/ supplies are prepared and are readily available for use.	_____	c. Participating in cooperative learning groups.	_____
		d. Allowing all students to answer questions.	_____
3. Planning provides for differentiation of instruction.	_____	3. Instructional time is used wisely.	_____
4. Planning provides for active student involvement.	_____	4. Differentiation of instruction is evident.	_____
5. Teacher is using the curriculum from the textual materials being used, teacher's guide, concept/ skill being taught, or from visibly seeing the state frameworks being used or cited in lesson plans.	_____	5. When asked, the students know the skill or objective they are learning.	_____
		6. Instruction reflects use of curriculum guides.	_____

Management		Communication	
1. The classroom is a positive environment that encourages learning.	_____	1. Teacher directions and communications are clear.	_____
		2. The teacher models professional oral communication.	_____
2. Teacher communication is respectful.	_____	3. The teacher models professional written communication.	_____
3. Students are on task.	_____		
4. Time is well managed.	_____		
5. Transitions are managed in an efficient manner.	_____		

Comments:

Administrator Signature: _____

*Note: All indicators may not be observed during a walk-through visit.

SAMPLE SUPERINTENDENT'S FIVE-MINUTE WALK-THROUGH CHECKLIST

School:
Date:
Observer:

Observation: Overview	Yes	No
1. Is there evidence of current student work and student writing in the hallways?		
2. Are staff members engaged in their work and with students?		
3. Is the building clean?		
4. Does office staff greet individuals (students and adults) when they enter or call?		
5. Is the climate positive? Are staff members friendly to others they pass in the halls?		
6. Are students in classrooms visibly engaged in instruction by participating in discussions, completing class work, interacting with students about class work, or actively listening to the teacher?		
7. Is the disciplining of students clearly visible to those visiting the building? (Students being yelled at, students sitting on the floor in the hall in time out, etc.)		
8. Are doors closed and windows covered preventing you from observing in the classroom?		
9. Are parents/community members or volunteers visible in the school?		
10. When asked, do students know what skill or concept they are learning and the objective of the assignment they are completing?		

Comments:

_____

_____

_____

LEADERSHIP STAFF MAP

The Principal Demonstrates Leadership Capacity By...

Principal	MAP Score		Effectively builds relationships with staff, students, families and external community partners (Engagement)	Plans for School Improvement and monitors staff performance effectively (Instruction)	Understands and utilizes data by teacher and student and provides effective instructional interventions (Assessment)	Effectively manages discipline and integrates intervention models (Management)	Schedules staff effectively and builds leadership capacity (Builds leadership capacity)	Utilizes resources effectively (Budget, facilities, human capital) (Operational Management)
	CA	Math						
Principal 1	16	10	Some	Low	Low	Low	Some	Low
Principal 2	90	77	Strong	Strong	Some	Strong	Some	Low
Principal 3	32	16	Some	Some	Some	Low	Low	Low
Principal 4	37	15	Strong	Low	Low	Some	Some	Low
Principal 5	26	16	Some	Low	Low	Low	Low	Low
Principal 6	21	11	Low	Low	Low	Low	Low	Low

Key

Red = Low, Yellow = Low to Moderate, Green = Strong

Sample Action Plan

Primary Goal: Students will meet the academic growth requirements in 8 of 16 subgroups across Communication Arts and Math on the SY13 Adequate Yearly Progress (AYP) report.

Secondary Goal: At least 37% of tested students will score proficient or above on the year end state assessments in Communication Arts.

Description of Proposed Action/Activity (What is going to be done to address this goal?)	Rationale For Activity (Explain what data source justify this activity)	Results/ Measurement (What will be the evidence of completion of the activity?)	Person(s) Responsible (Who will be accountable for action/ activity?)	Resources	Timeline/ Completion (When will the activity occur and be complete?)	Strategic Plan Alignment (Reference Number)
Activity #1 of 2: School principals implement a state test action plan to improve performance at each school	See test scores	Action Plans	Curriculum Supervisor School Principals	See state test scores Professional Development	February 2012	1 and 3
Professional Development: Implement a ten-week professional development plan to improve teacher pedagogy focusing on academic vocabulary and increasing rigor in the classroom.	See state test scores	PD agendas, minutes, pre and post test scores, state test scores	Professional Development Supervisor	Stipends Instructional Materials	February 2012	1 and 3

Instructional Support and Educational Accountability Office
Instructional Update

COUNTDOWN: 9 INSTRUCTIONAL DAYS UNTIL THE APRIL 2ND TESTING WINDOW BEGINS

March 20, 2012
Destination Accreditation!
School Staff and Student Highlights

Seven Schools remained open for a Spring Break Camp last week. Those schools are commended for the extra energy during Spring Break to creatively target the MAP. The television news media reported on the camps last week and our Communications Department highlighted those schools on the district web page. Congratulations to the Spring Break Camp staff on successfully implementing a Spring Break Camp impacting hundreds of students across the district.

We hope everyone had a wonderful Spring Break. We have copied some of the MAP/EOC information from prior Instructional Updates in this Instructional Update for you to use as we get closer to the MAP/EOC tests. Thank you for your continued focused energy and positive attitude as we prepare to show the community that improvement in academics is occurring. If there are topics you want us to discuss during our staff MAP/EOC breakfast next week, please forward those to [ ].

MAP/EOC (Some information copied from previous updates)

Below is information from past updates to remind you about MAP/ EOC information. Based on the mock EOC data, predictive EOC scores were not what we had hoped they would be. It will be imperative that schools implement creative test prep strategies and ensure teachers and students remain focused and motivated.

Central Office is here to support you. Some recent MAP activities include:

-Staff development sessions have been held.
-Spring Break Camp occurred at some school sites.
-MAP prep materials were distributed for math.
-A count down is posted.
-MAP posters were distributed to schools.
-A parent meeting to distribute MAP information was held this week.
-The MAP resource link and released items are posted on our web page.
-MAP activities for families are being promoted through our web page.

Please let us know if there are any other supports that you need!
Collectively, we can show improvement this year.

Curriculum Audit

A curriculum audit team completed the curriculum audit two weeks ago, and they will be giving us guidance on the needed curriculum changes as we finish writing the curriculum for every content area. We will share the feedback on changes with you when we receive that information. We especially thank the curriculum staff for taking time to pull together all of the curriculum documents and for being available for the curriculum audit team to address any questions for the audit. Their work on this in a short time frame was outstanding!

Data Samples

ATTENDANCE

	Attend. 2005-2006	Attend. 2006-2007	Attend. 2007-2008	Attend. 2008-2009
Benchmark	**94.00%**	**94.00%**	**94.00%**	**94.00%**
Division				
All Stus	95.36%	95.05%	94.75%	94.86%
Black Stus	95.30%	94.39%	94.61%	94.76%
Hispanic Stus	95.25%	94.88%	95.57%	94.76%
White Stus	95.31%	95.03%	94.64%	94.81%
Lim Engl Prof	95.73%	96.15%	96.05%	95.80%
Disadv Stus	93.22%	92.93%	92.23%	92.65%
Stus w/ Disab	93.31%	93.09%	92.70%	92.57%
School 1				
All Stus	95.77%	95.92%	95.86%	96.01%
Black Stus	97.65%	98.97%	97.97%	96.41%
Hispanic Stus	95.62%	96.02%	96.06%	95.46%
White Stus	95.73%	95.88%	95.83%	96.01%
Lim Engl Prof	92.00%	95.73%	95.98%	96.18%
Disadv Stus	94.54%	94.89%	94.64%	94.69%
Stus w/ Disab	95.09%	95.25%	95.07%	94.44%

Sample Subgroup Performance Tracker

SCHOOL DISTRICT'S NAME REMOVED

	English Perf. 2005-2006	English Perf. 2006-2007	EnglishPerf. 2007-2008	EnglishPerf. 2008-2009
Benchmark	65.00%	69.00%	73.00%	77.00%
Division				
All Stus	77.18%	81.27%	83.38%	86.08%
Black Stus	62.23%	67.92%	67.77%	71.47%
Hispanic Stus	71.73%	82.50%	78.88%	83.01%
White Stus	77.91%	81.90%	84.37%	86.88%
Lim Engl Prof	76.08%	83.33%	87.15%	85.95%
Disadv Stus	58.18%	66.78%	68.26%	73.89%
Stus w/ Disab	46.02%	55.42%	57.50%	67.77%
School 1				
All Stus	80.66%	86.11%	87.30%	89.96%
Black Stus	100.00%	100.00%	100.00%	33.33%
Hispanic Stus	100.00%	100.00%	100.00%	75.00%
White Stus	80.11%	85.77%	86.93%	90.76%
Lim Engl Prof	N/A	100.00%	100.00%	100.00%
Disadv Stus	70.76%	83.51%	78.82%	82.72%
Stus w/ Disab	30.76%	90.90%	83.33%	78.57%
School 2				
All Stus	60.60%	69.44%	72.00%	88.98%
Black Stus	42.85%	0.00%	50.00%	100.00%
Hispanic Stus	N/A	100.00%	N/A	N/A
White Stus	62.71%	69.56%	71.73%	88.07%
Lim Engl Prof	N/A	N/A	N/A	N/A
Disadv Stus	21.73%	41.02%	55.81%	85.00%

Annual Performance Report Projections (sample blank chart to track district's students)

Standard	2012 Target	Best Case Projection	Goal	SY11 Actual	Nov. 2011 Projected	Feb. 2012 Projected		Data Used for Projection	# of additional students Needed
9.1*1 - 3-5 Math									
9.1*2 - 3-5 Comm. Arts									
9.4*1 - Advanced Courses									
9.6 – Attend.									

Sample School Based Graph to Examine Reading Scores
School and Student Names Removed for Confidentiality

2ⁿᵈ GRADE DRA SCORES

Student	Sept.	Dec.	March
Averages:	11.4	16.5	21.9
Student 1	8	12	16
Student 2	8	16	24
Student 3	6	10	14
Student 4	10	24	30
Student 5	16	28	
Student 6	12	16	20
Student 7	24	24	40
Student 8	12	16	20
Student 9	14	18	24
Student 10	24	28	34
Student 11	8	12	18
Student 12	4	8	12
Student 13	6	8	16
Student 14	18	24	30
Sudent 15	16	20	28
Student 16	4	8	12
Student 17	4	8	12

Sample Graphs to Look at Achievement Gaps for African American Students

District Name Removed for Confidentiality

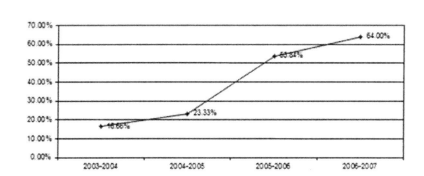

Elementary School Closes Achievement Gap for Special Education Students

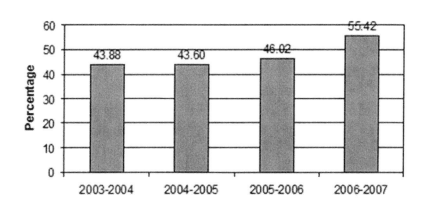

School ABC

TEACHER GROWTH CHART

The chart can be used to look at growth across a school, across a grade level or across a district. Highlight declines in red, positive growth in green and no change in yellow.

The data below is extracted from actual teacher's scores in a school. As an exercise, give your administrators the teacher growth data chart for their school and facilitate a discussion. Have principals repeat this activity with their teachers by giving the grade level team the growth data for the grade level and facilitate a grade level discussion.

School	Teacher	Content	Grade	# Tested	%Proficient/ Advanced Year 1 (2011)	%Proficient/ Advanced Year 2 (2012)	%Growth/ Decline	Goal
ABC	Sally	English	3	25	30%	15%	-15%	65%
ABC	Patty	English	3	25	25%	25%	0%	65%
ABC	Michelle	English	3	25	50%	60%	+10%	65%
ABC	Corrine	English	3	25	40%	60%	+20%	65%
ABC	Sally	Math	3	25	50%	60%	+10	75%
ABC	Patty	Math	3	25	30%	40%	+10	75%
ABC	Michelle	Math	3	25	60%	75%	+15%	75%
ABC	Corrine	Math	3	25	80%	80%	0%	75%

REFLECTIVE DISCUSSION QUESTIONS

1. What can you conclude from the data?
2. What are the strengths within the team?
3. What are the challenge areas?
4. How many students would you need to reach the goal?
5. What strategies were used in 2011 that may have impacted 2012?
6. How can the team capitalize on the strengths within the grade level?
7. What are the best practices and what's the pacing chart for Corrine and Michelle?
8. How are Michelle and Corrine's best practices being replicated?

9. Have the teachers observed each other or taped lessons for each other to look at strategies?
10. What are the reading strategies and materials used in the lower performing classes compared to the others?

Recent Edtrust Recognized High Performing, High Minority School Districts

The following school districts have implemented a culture of high achievement. While some schools perform better than others, there are numerous schools within each of these districts that are highly successful urban public schools. The leadership style of the principals and superintendent may vary, but they are many commonalities in the emphasis on relationships, pedagogy, and curriculum that are beneficial for other educators to study and replicate.

1. Charlotte Mecklenburg - Virginia
2. Miami-Dade County Public Schools – Florida
3. San Francisco Unified, California
4. Gwinnett County Public Schools
5. Brownsville Independent School District
6. Norfolk Public Schools, VA
7. Fontana Unified School District, CA
8. Palm Beach County - Florida
9. Houston Independent School District - Texas
10. Corona-Norco – California

High Performing Charter School Organizations

While all of the schools within each of the organizations below are not high performing, there are multiple schools within each of the charter organizations below that are high performing.

1. KIPP
2. YES College Preparatory
3. Uncommon Schools

High Performing High Minority or High Poverty Public and Private Schools (Non-Charter)

1. Frankford Elementary School, Frankford, Delaware
2. Rock Hall Elementary School, Rock Hall, Maryland
3. Central Elementary School, Paintsville, KY
4. Hambrick Middle School, Houston, TX
5. Lapwai Elementary School, Lapwai, ID
6. PS 12, Brooklyn, New York
7. Science Park High School, Newark, New Jersey
8. Elizabeth High School, Union, New Jersey
9. Metro High School, St. Louis Missouri
10. Kennard Classical Academy, ST. Louis Missouri
11. Bay School District, Florida
12. Calhoun School District, Florida
13. Ron Clark Academy (Private), Atlanta, Georgia
14. Norview High School, Norfolk, VA
15. West Jasper Elementary School, Jasper, AL
16. Garden Grove Unified School District, Garden Grove, CA
17. Aldine Independent School District, Aldine, TX
18. Boston Public Schools, Boston, MA
19. Charlotte-Mecklenburg Schools Charlotte, NC
20. Norfolk Public Schools, Norfolk, VA
21. Garden Grove Unified School District, CA
22. Jefferson County Public Schools, KY
23. Long Beach Unified School District, CA
24. Longfellow Elementary School, Mount Vernon, NY
25. St. James - Gaillard Elementary School, Orangeburg County, SC
26. Sycamore Elementary School, Kokomo, IN
27. Lincoln Elementary School, Mount Vernon, NY
28. Jim Thorpe Fundamental School, Santa Ana Unified School District, CA
29. R.N. Harris Integrated Arts, Durham Public Schools, NC

30. Jim Thorpe Fundamental School, Santa Ana Unified School District, CA
31. R.N. Harris Integrated Arts, Durham Public Schools, NC
32. Samuel W. Tucker Elementary School, Alexandria, VA
33. Centennial Place Elementary School, Atlanta, GA
34. David D. Jones Elementary School, Guilford County, NC
35. South Scotland Elementary School, Scotland County, NC
36. The Young Women's Leadership School of East Harlem, New York, NY
37. Lincoln College Prep, Kansas City, Missouri
38. West Manor Elementary School, Atlanta, GA
39. Frankford Elementary School, Frankford, DE
40. University Park Campus School, Worcester, MA
41. Elmont Memorial Junior-Senior High School, Elmont, NY
42. Dayton's Bluff Elementary School, St. Paul, MN
43. Kennard Classical Junior Academy, St. Louis Missouri
44. Lincoln College Prep, Kansas City, Missouri
45. Truman Elementary, St. Louis, Missouri

2011 National Blue Ribbon Schools and Their Contact Information.

This list is from the US Department of Education

ALABAMA

Barkley Bridge Elementary
School
2333 Barkley Bridge Road
Hartselle, AL 35640-3876
Phone: (256) 773-1931

Oak Mountain High School
5476 Caldwell Mill Road
Birmingham, AL 35242-4520
Phone: (205) 682-5200

Our Lady of the Valley Catholic
School (Private)
5510 Double Oak Lane
Birmingham, AL 35242-3513
Phone: (205) 991-5963

Phillips Preparatory School
3255 Old Shell Road
Mobile, AL 36607-2504
Phone: (251) 221-2286

Thelma Smiley Morris
Elementary School
801 Hill Street
Montgomery, AL 36108-2713
Phone: (334) 223-6920

ALASKA

Chugach Optional Elementary
School
1205 East Street
Anchorage, AK 99501-4499
Phone: (907) 742-3730

Unalaska Junior/Senior High
School
55 East Broadway
P.O. Box 570
Unalaska, AK 99685-0570
Phone: (907) 581-1222

ARIZONA

Franklin East Elementary School
1753 East 8th Avenue
Mesa, AZ 85204-3617
Phone: (480) 472-6431

Franklin Phonetic Primary
School
6116 East Highway 69
Prescott Valley, AZ 86314-2806
Phone: (928) 775-6747

ARKANSAS

Bellview Elementary School
5400 South Bellview Road
Rogers, AR 72758-8871
Phone: (479) 631-3605

Jim Stone Elementary School
4255 College Avenue
Conway, AR 72034-7276
Phone: (501) 450-4808

CALIFORNIA

California Academy of
Mathematics and Science
1000 East Victoria Street
Carson, CA 90747-0001
Phone: (310) 243-2025

Ethan B. Allen Elementary
School
16200 Bushard Street
Fountain Valley, CA 92708-1505
Phone: (714) 663-6228

James Leitch Elementary School
47100 Fernald Street
Fremont, CA 94539-7005
Phone: (510) 657-6100

Jim Thorpe Fundamental School
2450 West Alton
Santa Ana, CA 92704-7118
Phone: (714) 430-5800

Los Penasquitos Elementary
School
14125 Cuca Street
San Diego, CA 92129-1852
Phone: (858) 672-3600

Miramonte Elementary School
1590 Bellaire Avenue
Clovis, CA 93611-5103
Phone: (559) 327-7400

Ruskin Elementary School
1401 Turlock Lane
San Jose, CA 95132-2347
Phone: (408) 923-1950

Sanger Academy Charter School
2207 Ninth Street
Sanger, CA 93657-9666
Phone: (559) 524-6840

Santa Fe Christian Lower School
838 Academy Drive
Solana Beach, CA 92075-2034
Phone: (858) 755-8900

Ulloa Elementary School
2650 42nd Avenue
San Francisco, CA 94116-2714
Phone: (415) 759-2841

CONNECTICUT

Brownstone Intermediate School
314 Main Street
Portland, CT 06480-1877
Phone: (860) 342-6765

Helen Keller Middle School
360 Sport Hill Road
Easton, CT 06612-1651
Phone: (203) 261-3607

Kelly Lane Intermediate School
60 Kelly Lane
Granby, CT 06035-2920
Phone: (860) 844-3041

Middlebrook School
131 School Road
Wilton, CT 06897-2528
Phone: (203) 762-8388

Saint Gabriel School
77 Bloomfield Avenue
Windsor, CT 06095-2811
Phone: (860) 688-6401

DELAWARE

Long Neck Elementary School
26064 School Lane
Millsboro, DE 19966-0902
Phone: (302) 945-6200

DEPARTMENT OF DEFENSE

West Point Middle School
705 Barry Road
West Point, NY 10996-1196
Phone: (845) 938-2923

District of Columbia

Horace Mann Elementary School
4430 Newark Street, NW
Washington, DC 20016-2737
Phone: (202) 282-0126

FLORIDA

Archimedean Academy
12425 Southwest 72nd Street
Miami, FL 33183-2513
Phone: (305) 279-6572

Archimedean Middle
Conservatory School
12425 Southwest 72nd Street
Miami, FL 33183-2513
Phone: (305) 276-6572

Christ the King Catholic School
3809 Morrison Avenue
Tampa, FL 33629-4436
Phone: (813) 876-8770

Dr. N.H. Jones Elementary
Magnet School
1900 SW 5th Street
Ocala, FL 34471-1861
Phone: (352) 671-7260

Ethel Koger Beckham Elementary
School
4702 Southwest 143 Court
Miami, FL 33175-6893
Phone: (305) 222-8161

Queen of Peace Catholic
Academy
10900 S.W. 24th Avenue
Gainesville, FL 32607-1207
Phone: (352) 332-8808

Saint Martha Catholic School
(Private School)
4380 Fruitville Road
Sarasota, FL 34232-1623
Phone: (941) 953-4181

St. Paul's Catholic School
428 2nd Avenue North
Jacksonville Beach, FL
32250-5597
Phone: (904) 249-5934

The Samuel Scheck Hillel
Community Day
School | The Ben Lipson Hillel
Community
High School
19000 NE 25th Avenue
North Miami Beach, FL
33180-3209
Phone: (305) 931-2831

GEORGIA

Big Creek Elementary School
1994 Peachtree Parkway
Cumming, GA 30041-9506
Phone: (770) 887-4584

Fulton Science Academy
1675 Hembree Road
Alpharetta, GA 30009-2083
Phone: (770) 753-4141

Our Lady of the Assumption
Catholic School
1320 Hearst Drive NE
Atlanta, GA 30319-2711
Phone: (404) 364-1902

Peachtree City Elementary
School
201 Wisdom Road
Peachtree City, GA 30269-1128
Phone: (770) 631-3250

Savannah Christian Preparatory
School –
Lower School
1599 Chatham Parkway
Savannah, GA 31402-2848
Phone: (912) 234-1653

Timber Ridge Elementary School
5000 Timber Ridge Road
Marietta, GA 30068-1529
Phone: (770) 642-5621

HAWAII

King Liholiho Elementary School
3430 Maunaloa Avenue
Honolulu, HI 96816-3795
Phone: (808) 733-4850

Koko Head Elementary School
189 Lunalilo Home Road
Honolulu, HI 96825-2099
Phone: (808) 397-5811

IDAHO

Ponderosa Elementary School
3483 Ponderosa Road
P.O. Box 40
Post Falls, ID 83877-9613
Phone: (208) 773-1508

ILLINOIS

Carlinville Primary School
18456 Shipman Road
Carlinville, IL 62626-2442
Phone: (217) 854-9849

Epiphany Catholic School
1002 East College Avenue
Normal, IL 61761-3129
Phone: (309) 452-3268

Greenbrier Elementary School
2330 N. Verde Drive
Arlington Heights, IL
60004-2867
Phone: (847) 398-4272

Highland Elementary School
3935 Highland Avenue
Downers Grove, IL 60515-1515
Phone: (630) 719-5835

The Lane Elementary School
500 N. Elm Street
Hinsdale, IL 60521-3519
Phone: (630) 887-1430

Lincoln Magnet School
300 S. 11th Street
Springfield, IL 62703-1204
Phone: (217) 525-3236

Mary, Seat of Wisdom Catholic
School
1352 S. Cumberland Avenue
Park Ridge, IL 60068-5121
Phone: (847) 825-2500

Northside College Preparatory
High School
5501 N. Kedzie Avenue
Chicago, IL 60625-3923
Phone: (773) 534-3954

Queen of the Rosary School
690 Elk Grove Boulevard
Elk Grove Village, IL
60007-4262
Phone: (847) 437-3322

Robert Frost Junior High School
320 W. Wise Road
Schaumburg, IL 60193-0000
Phone: (847) 357-6800

St. Emily School
1400 E. Central Road
Mount Prospect, IL 60056-2650
Phone: (847) 296-3490

Saint Joan of Arc School
4913 Columbia Avenue
Lisle, IL 60532-3503
Phone: (630) 969-1732

Saint Linus School
10400 S. Lawler Avenue
Oak Lawn, IL 60453-4717
Phone: (708) 425-1656

St. Paul of the Cross School
140 S. Northwest Highway
Park Ridge, IL 60068-4253
Phone: (847) 825-6366

St. Therese Chinese Catholic
School
247 West 23rd Street
Chicago, IL 60616-1996
Phone: (312) 326-2837

Wood Oaks Junior High School
1250 Sanders Road
Northbrook, IL 60062-2906
Phone: (847) 272-1900

INDIANA

Benjamin Banneker
Achievement Center
301 Parke Street
Gary, IN 46403-2178
Phone: (219) 776-4027

Central Elementary School
515 E. Williams Street
Lebanon, IN 46052-2259
Phone: (765) 482-2000

Chrisney Elementary School
311 Church Street
Chrisney, IN 47611-0311
Phone: (812) 362-8200

Dwight D. Eisenhower
Elementary School
1450 S. Main Street
Crown Point, IN 46307-8444
Phone: (219) 663-8800

Fishers Elementary School
11442 Lantern Road
Fishers, IN 46038-0216
Phone: (317) 594-4160

Happy Hollow Elementary
School
1200 North Salisbury Street
West Lafayette, IN 46038-0216
Phone: (765) 746-0500

Otwell Elementary School
1869 N. State Road 257
P.O. Box 38
Otwell, IN 47564-0038
Phone: (812) 354-2600

St. Joseph Grade School
216 North Hill Street
South Bend, IN 46617-2720
Phone: (574) 234-0451

William Henry Burkhart
Elementary School
5701 Brill Road
Indianapolis, IN 46227-1908
Phone: (317) 789-3600

IOWA

Anita Elementary School
709 McIntyre Drive
Anita, IA 50020-1119
Phone: (712) 762-3231

Decorah High School
100 Claiborne Drive
Decorah, IA 52101-1400
Phone: (563) 382-3643

Greene Elementary School
210 West South Street
PO Box 190
Greene, IA 50636-0190
Phone: (641) 816-5629

MOC-Floyd Valley High School
615 8th Street SE
Orange City, IA 51041-1901
Phone: (712) 737-4871

St. Columbkille Elementary
School
1198 Rush Street
Dubuque, IA 52003-7599
Phone: (563) 582-3532

Saint Paul the Apostle Catholic
School
1007 E. Rusholme
Davenport, IA 52803-2596
Phone: (563) 322-2923

Washington Elementary School
610 Maiden Lane
Muscatine, IA 52761-2956
Phone: (563) 263-9135

KANSAS

Louisburg High School
202 Aquatic Drive
P.O. Box 399
Louisburg, KS 66053-0399
Phone: (913) 837-1720

MacArthur Elementary School
925 S. Holly Drive
Liberal, KS 67901-2050
Phone: (620) 604-1700

Oswego High School
1501 Tomahawk Trail
Oswego, KS 67356-0129
Phone: (620) 795-2125

Sunflower Elementary School
775 North Center
Gardner, KS 66030-1770
Phone: (913) 856-3700

Union Valley Elementary School
2501 E. 30th
Hutchinson, KS 67502-1231
Phone: (620) 662-4891

KENTUCKY

Gamaliel Elementary School
320 East Main Street
Gamaliel, KY 42140-0200
Phone: (270) 457-2341

Mary Queen of the Holy Rosary
School
605 Hill N. Dale Drive
Lexington, KY 40503-2116
Phone: (859) 277-3030

North Middletown Elementary
School
301 College Street North
P.O. Box 67
North Middletown, KY
40361-9509
Phone: (859) 362-4523

Southside Elementary School
170 State Highway 319
P.O. Box 500
Belfry, KY 41514-0500
Phone: (606) 353-7296

W.R. McNeill Elementary School
1800 Creason Drive
Bowling Green, KY 42101-3551
Phone: (270) 746-2260

Woodfill Elementary School
1025 Alexandria Pike
Ft. Thomas, KY 41075-2519
Phone: (859) 441-0506

LOUISIANA

Eden Gardens Fundamental
Elementary School
626 Eden Boulevard
Shreveport, LA 71106-5199
Phone: (318) 861-7654

Hattie A. Watts Elementary
School
1307 Third Street
Patterson, LA 70392-5049
Phone: (985) 395-5976

Louisiana School for Math,
Science, and the Arts
715 University Parkway
Natchitoches, LA 71457-9990
Phone: (318) 357-2525

Metairie Academy for Advanced
Studies
201 Metairie Road
Metairie, LA 70005-4538
Phone: (504) 833-5539

Rosenthal Montessori
Elementary School
1951 Monroe Street
Alexandria, LA 71301-6673
Phone: (318) 442-5791

Maine

Eliot Elementary School
1298 State Road
Eliot, ME 03903-1319
Phone: (207) 439-9004

Orono Middle School
14 Goodridge Drive
Orono, ME 04473-1494
Phone: (207) 866-2350

Maryland

Bel Air Elementary School
14401 Barton Boulevard
Cumberland, MD 21502-5899
Phone: (301) 729-2992

Lime Kiln Middle School
11650 Scaggsville Road
Fulton, MD 20759-2208
Phone: (410) 880-5988

Mary of Nazareth Roman
Catholic School (Private School)
14131 Seneca Road
Darnestown, MD 20874-3337
Phone: (301) 869-0940

Oklahoma Road Middle School
6300 Oklahoma Road
Sykesville, MD 21874-6604
Phone: (410) 751-3600

St. Bartholomew Catholic School
6900 River Road
Bethesda, MD 20817-4744
Phone: (301) 229-5586

St. Jane de Chantal Catholic
School
9525 Old Georgetown Road
Bethesda, MD 20814-1796
Phone: (301) 530-1221

Saint Mary's School
600 Veirs Mill Road
Rockville, MD 20852-1139
Phone: (301) 762-4179

Severna Park High School
60 Robinson Road
Severna Park, MD 21146-2899
Phone: (410) 544-0900

Towson High School Law and
Public Policy
69 Cedar Avenue
Towson, MD 21286-7844
Phone: (410) 887-3608

MASSACHUSETTS

Boston Latin School
78 Avenue Louis Pasteur
Boston, MA 02115-5744
Phone: (617) 635-8895

Sharon High School
181 Pond Street
Sharon, MA 02067-2000
Phone: (781) 784-1554

MINNESOTA

Atheneum Elementary School
5899 Babcock Trail
Inver Grove Heights, MN
55077-3232
Phone: (651) 582-8786

Brandon Elementary School
206 West Third Street
Brandon, MN 56315-0185
Phone: (651) 582-8786

Highlands Elementary School
5505 Doncaster Way
Edina, MN 55436-2017
Phone: (651) 582-8786

Randolph Elementary School
29110 Davisson Avenue
Randolph, MN 55065-0038
Phone: (651) 582-8786

Viking Elementary School
305 Melgaard Avenue
Viking, MN 56760-0010
Phone: (651) 582-8786

West Central Area South
Elementary School
31 Central Avenue North
Kensington, MN 56343-0000
Phone: (651) 582-8786

MISSISSIPPI

Kathleen Bankston Elementary
School
1312 Grand Boulevard
Greenwood, MS 38930-2214
Phone: (662) 455-7421

North Bay Elementary School
1825 Popp's Ferry Road
Biloxi, MS 39532-2227
Phone: (228) 435-6166

MISSOURI

Crestwood Elementary School
1020 S. Sappington Road
St. Louis, MO 63126-1005
Phone: (314) 729-2430

Roosevelt Elementary School
1040 Forster Street
Farmington, MO 63640-2604
Phone: (573) 701-1345

MONTANA

Cold Springs School
2625 Briggs Street
Missoula, MT 59801-1099
Phone: (406) 542-4010

Russell Elementary School
3216 Russell Street
Missoula, MT 59801-8537
Phone: (406) 542-4080

NEBRASKA

Alma Elementary School
515 Jewell Street
P.O. Box 170
Alma, NE 68920-0170
Phone: (308) 928-2131

NEVADA

Advanced Technologies
Academy
2501 Vegas Drive
Las Vegas, NV 89106-1643
Phone: (702) 799-7870

NEW HAMPSHIRE

Sandown North Elementary
School
23 Stagecoach Drive
Sandown, NH 03873-2123
Phone: (603) 887-8503

NEW JERSEY

Holy Trinity Interparochial
School
336 First Street
Westfield, NJ 07090-3318
Phone: (908) 233-0484

Lincoln Elementary School
712 Lincoln Avenue
Ridgefield Park, NJ 07660-1416
Phone: (201) 994-1830

New Providence High School
35 Pioneer Drive
New Providence, NJ
07974-1575
Phone: (908) 464-4700

Our Lady of Mercy Academy
25 Fremont Avenue
Park Ridge, NJ 07656-2036
Phone: (201) 391-3838

Our Lady of the Lake School
(Private School)
26 Lakeside Avenue
Verona, NJ 07044-1819
Phone: (973) 239-1160

Rumson-Fair Haven Regional
High School
74 Ridge Road
Rumson, NJ 07760-1896
Phone: (732) 842-1597

Saint Elizabeth School
Greenwood Avenue
Wyckoff, NJ 07481-1519
Phone: (201) 891-1481

St. John the Apostle School
825 Valley Road
Clark, NJ 07066-1901
Phone: (732) 388-1360

Saint John's Academy
460 Hillsdale Avenue
Hillsdale, NJ 07642-2713
Phone: (201) 664-6364

St. Joseph School
305 Elm Street
Oradell, NJ 07649-2293
Phone: (201) 261-2388

Terence C. Reilly School No. 7
436 First Avenue
Elizabeth, NJ 07206-1122
Phone: (908) 436-6030

Tewksbury Elementary School
109 Fairmount Road East
Califon, NJ 07830-3199
Phone: (908) 832-2594

Thomas Jefferson Elementary
School
233 Goffle Hill Road
Hawthorne, NJ 07506-3213
Phone: (973) 423-6480

Watchung School
4 Garden Street
Montclair, NJ 07042-4198
Phone: (973) 509-4259

New Mexico

Griegos Elementary School
4040 San Isidro NW
Albuquerque, NM 87107-2828
Phone: (505) 345-3661

New York

Beacon School of Excellence
825 4th Avenue
Brooklyn, NY 11232-1701
Phone: (718) 965-4200

Clarke Middle School
740 Edgewood Drive
Westbury, NY 11590-5409
Phone: (516) 876-7401

Eagle Hill Middle School
4645 Enders Road
Manlius, NY 13104-8702
Phone: (315) 692-1400

Early Childhood School for
Science &
Technology P.S. 130 Q
200-01 42nd Avenue
Bayside, NY 11361-1896
Phone: (718) 357-6606

Forest Park Elementary School
30 Deforest Road
Dix Hills, NY 11746-4808
Phone: (631) 592-3550

French Road Elementary School
488 French Road
Rochester, NY 14618-5373
Phone: (585) 242-5140

Mildred E. Strang Middle School
2701 Crompond Road
Yorktown Heights, NY
10598-3129
Phone: (914) 243-8100

Northeast School
425 Winthrop Drive
Ithaca, NY 14850-8606
Phone: (607) 257-2121

Oldfield Middle School
2 Oldfield Road
Greenlawn, NY 11740-1235
Phone: (631) 754-5310

William G. Wilcox School
1055 Targee Street
Staten Island, NY 10304-4450
Phone: (718) 447-8323

Queens Elementary School
205-01 33rd Avenue
Bayside, NY 11361-1029
Phone: (718) 423-8553

Fresh Meadow School
174-10 67th Avenue
Flushing, NY 11365-2031
Phone: (718) 358-2243

Pearl River Middle School
520 Gilbert Ave.
Pearl River, NY 10965-3320
Phone: (845) 620-3870

Pine Brook Elementary School
2300 English Road
Rochester, NY 14616-1682
Phone: (585) 966-4600

Red Mill Elementary School
225 McCullough Place
Rensselaer, NY 12144-3718
Phone: (518) 207-2660

Saint Ignatius Loyola School
48 East 84th Street
New York, NY 10028-0806
Phone: (212) 861-3820

Sheridan Hill Elementary School
4560 Boncrest Drive East
Williamsville, NY 14221-6304
Phone: (716) 407-9250

Transfiguration Roman Catholic
School
29 Mott Street
New York, NY 10013-5006
Phone: (212) 962-5265

Willets Road School
455 I.U. Willets Road
Roslyn Heights, NY 11577-2823
Phone: (516) 333-8797

NORTH CAROLINA

Brown Summit Middle School
Center for
Advanced Academics
4720 NC Highway 150 East
Brown Summit, NC 27214-9551
Phone: (336) 656-0432

Collettsville School
4690 Collettsville School Road
Collettsville, NC 28611-9138
Phone: (828) 754-6913

The Franciscan School
10000 St. Francis Drive
Raleigh, NC 27613-5954
Phone: (919) 847-8205

Metrolina Regional Scholars
Academy
5225 Seventy-seven Center
Drive
Charlotte, NC 28217-0708
Phone: (704) 503-1112

Piedmont Open Middle School
1241 E. 10th Street
Charlotte, NC 28204-2048
Phone: (980) 343-5435

Quest Academy Charter School
10908 Strickland Road
Raleigh, NC 27615-2082
Phone: (919) 841-0441

Ohio

All Saints School
8939 Montgomery Road
Cincinnati, OH 45236-2129
Phone: (513) 792-4732

Cardington-Lincoln Elementary
School
121 Nichols Street
Cardington, OH 43315-1121
Phone: (419) 864-6692

Citizens Academy
1827 Ansel Road
Cleveland, OH 44106-4107
Phone: (216) 791-4195

Kensington Intermediate School
20140 Lake Road
Rocky River, OH 44116-3980
Phone: (440) 356-6770

Kings Mills Elementary School
1780 King Avenue
P.O. Box 912
Kings Mills, OH 45034-1720
Phone: (513) 398-8050

Lake Elementary School
225 Lincoln Street
Hartville, OH 44632-9382
Phone: (330) 877-4276

Maplewood Elementary School
1699 Kinsman Road NE
North Bloomfield, OH
44450-9700
Phone: (330) 583-2321

Putman Elementary School
327 E. Baldwin Street
Blanchester, OH 45107-1203
Phone: (937) 783-3523

Saint Angela Merici School
20830 Lorain Road
Fairview Park, OH 44126-2096
Phone: (440) 333-2126

Saint Barnabas Catholic School
9200 Olde Eight Road
Northfield, OH 44067-2014
Phone: (330) 467-7921

St. Columban School
896 Oakland Road
Loveland, OH 45140-8484
Phone: (513) 683-7903

St. Francis Xavier School
612 East Washington Street
Medina, OH 44256-2182
Phone: (330) 725-3345

St. Joan of Arc School
498 East Washington Street
Chagrin Falls, OH 44022-2959
Phone: (440) 247-6530

South Range High School
11300 Columbiana-Canfield
Road, Suite H
Canfield, OH 44406-8485
Phone: (330) 549-2163

Springboro High School
1675 S. Main Street
Springboro, OH 45066-1524
Phone: (937) 748-3950

Timmons Elementary School
9595 East Washington Street
Chagrin Falls, OH 44023-2762
Phone: (440) 543-9380

Union Elementary School
390 W. Walker Street
Upper Sandusky, OH
43351-1364
Phone: (419) 294-5721

West Boulevard Elementary
School
6125 West Boulevard
Youngstown, OH 44512-5678
Phone: (330) 726-3427

OKLAHOMA

Belle Isle Enterprise Middle
School
5904 North Villa Avenue
Oklahoma City, OK 73112-7157
Phone: (405) 843-0888

Bishop Elementary School
2204 SW Bishop Road
Lawton, OK 73505-0876
Phone: (580) 353-4870

Carver Middle School
624 East Oklahoma Place
Tulsa, OK 74106-4831
Phone: (918) 925-1420

Cleveland Bailey Elementary
School
3301 Sun Valley
Midwest City, OK 73110-1399
Phone: (405) 739-1656

Deer Creek Prairie Vale
Elementary School
22522 North Pennsylvania
Avenue
Edmond, OK 73025-9100
Phone: (405) 359-3170

Gilmour Elementary School
1400 South Oak Street
Kingfisher, OK 73750-4314
Phone: (405) 375-4080

PENNSYLVANIA

Aiken Elementary School
881 Greentree Road
Pittsburgh, PA 15220-3400
Phone: (412) 571-6241

Central High School
1700 W. Olney Avenue
Philadelphia, PA 19141-1198
Phone: (215) 276-5262

Coebourn Elementary School
1 Coebourn Boulevard
Brookhaven, PA 19015-1641
Phone: (610) 497-6300

Corpus Christi Catholic School
920 Sumneytown Pike
Lansdale, PA 19446-0194
Phone: (215) 368-0582

Nativity of Our Lord School
585 W. Street Road
Warminster, PA 18974-3292
Phone: (215) 675-2820

New Eagle Elementary School
507 Pugh Road
Wayne, PA 19087-1906
Phone: (610) 240-1551

Pleasant Valley Elementary
School
250 East McMurray Road
McMurray, PA 15317-2948
Phone: (724) 941-6260

Pocopson Elementary School
1105 Pocopson Road
West Chester, PA 19382-7049
Phone: (610) 793-9241

Rose Tree Elementary School
1101 First Avenue
Media, PA 19063-1206
Phone: (610) 627-7201

RHODE ISLAND

Hope Valley Elementary School
15 Thelma Drive
Hope Valley, RI 02832-2421
Phone: (401) 539-2321

SOUTH CAROLINA

Holly Springs Elementary School
120 Holly Springs School Road
Pickens, SC 29671-9229
Phone: (864) 397-2000

Townville Elementary School
105 Townville School Rd
P.O. Box 10
Townville, SC 29689-0010
Phone: (864) 403-2600

TENNESSEE

Fairmont Elementary School
1405 Lester Harris Road
Johnson City, TN 37601-2673
Phone: (423) 434-5275

Frazier Elementary School
3900 Double S. Road
Dayton, TN 37321-5344
Phone: (423) 775-7854

Fred J. Page High School
6281 Amo Road
Franklin, TN 37064-7902
Phone: (615) 472-4730

Hume-Fogg Magnet High School
700 Broadway
Nashville, TN 37203-3900
Phone: (615) 291-6300

Morriston West High School
1 Trojan Trail
Morristown, TN 37813-5460
Phone: (423) 581-1600

TEXAS

Austin Middle School
1514 Avenue N. 1/2
Galveston, TX 77550-8198
Phone: (409) 761-3500

Challenge Early College High
School
5601 West Loop South
Houston, TX 77081-2221
Phone: (713) 664-9712

Dallas Environmental Science
Academy
3635 Greenleaf Street
Dallas, TX 75212-3747
Phone: (972) 794-3950

E. A. Lyons Elementary School
800 Roxella Road
Houston, TX 77076-4431
Phone: (713) 696-2870

Eastwood Academy High School
1315 Dumble Street
Houston, TX 77023-1902
Phone: (713) 924-1697

Hillcrest Elementary School
2611 Avenue H
Nederland, TX 77627-5029
Phone: (409) 722-3484

Irma Lerma Rangel Young
Women's Leadership School
1718 Robert B. Cullum Boulvard
Dallas, TX 75210-2550
Phone: (972) 749-5200

Lomax Elementary School
10615 North Avenue L
La Porte, TX 77571-6496
Phone: (281) 604-4300

Martin Elementary School
3500 Pine Street
Beaumont, TX 77703-3698
Phone: (409) 617-6425

Rising Star Elementary School
P.O. Box 37
Rising Star, TX 76471-0037
Phone: (254) 643-2431

Rosie Sorrells School of
Education and
Social Services
1201 E. Eighth Street
Dallas, TX 75203-2545
Phone: (972) 925-5940

School of Science and
Engineering Magnet
1201 E. Eighth Street
Dallas, TX 75203-2545
Phone: (972) 925-5964

Silva Magnet School for Health
Professions
121 Val Verde Street
El Paso, TX 79905-3945
Phone: (915) 533-9654

Westchester Academy for
International Studies
901 Yorkchester
Houston, TX 77079-3437
Phone: (713) 251-1800

YES Prep Southwest School
4411 Anderson Road
Houston, TX 77053-2307
Phone: (713) 413-0001

Utah

Milford Elementary School
450 South 700 West
PO Box 309
Milford, UT 84751-0309
Phone: (435) 387-2841

Virginia

Belmont Station Elementary
School
20235 Nightwatch Street
Ashburn, VA 20147-7463
Phone: (571) 252-2240

Kemps Landing Magnet School
4722 Jericho Road
Virginia Beach, VA 23462-2226
Phone: (757) 648-4650

Our Lady of Lourdes School
8250 Woodman Road
Richmond, VA 23228-3200
Phone: (804) 262-1770

Rich Acres Elementary School
400 Rich Acres School Road
Martinsville, VA 24112-0006
Phone: (276) 638-3366

Richmond Community High
School
201 E. Brookland Park Boulevard
Richmond, VA 23222-2722
Phone: (804) 780-4332

Rocky Mount Elementary School
555 School Board Road
Rocky Mount, VA 24151-6614
Phone: (540) 483-5040

St. Ann Catholic School
980 North Frederick Street
Arlington, VA 22205-2552
Phone: (703) 525-7599

Saint Matthew Catholic School
3316 Sandra Lane
Virginia Beach, VA 23464-1736
Phone: (757) 420-2455

St. Thomas Aquinas Regional
School
13750 Mary's Way
Woodbridge, VA 22191-2078
Phone: (703) 491-4447

Springville Elementary School
144 Schoolhouse Road
North Tazewell, VA 24630-7921
Phone: (276) 322-5900

Star of the Sea Catholic School
309 15th Street
Virginia Beach, VA 23451-3437
Phone: (757) 428-8400

WASHINGTON

Loyal Heights Elementary School
2511 NW 80th Street
Seattle, WA 98117-4497
Phone: (206) 252-1500

WEST VIRGINIA

Inwood Primary School
7864 Winchester Avenue
Inwood, WV 25428-4067
Phone: (304) 229-1990

Maxwell Hill Elementary School
1001 Maxwell Hill Road
Beckley, WV 25801-2457
Phone: (304) 256-4599

Triadelphia Middle School
1636 National Road
Wheeling, WV 26003-5598
Phone: (304) 243-0387

WISCONSIN

Fremont Elementary School
PO Box 308
Fremont, WI 54940-0308
Phone: (920) 867-8050

Paris Elementary School
1901 176th Avenue
Kenosha, WI 53144-7615
Phone: (262) 859-2350

Rib Lake High School
1200 North Street
PO Box 278
Rib Lake, WI 54470-0278
Phone: (715) 427-3220

Whittier Elementary School
4382 South Third Street
Milwaukee, WI 53207-4968
Phone: (414) 294-1400

WYOMING

Big Horn High School
333 US Hwy 335
P.O. Box 490
Big Horn, WY 82833-0490
Phone: (307) 674-8190

Gilchrist Elementary School
1108 Happy Jack Road
Cheyenne, WY 82009-8053
Phone: (307) 771-2285

Works Cited

(2012, March 12). Retrieved from Mabel B. Wesley Elementary School: http://www.wesleyelementary.org/

(2012, April 23). Retrieved from The Tripod Project: http://tripodproject.org/

History of Kennard Classical Junior Academy. (2012, March 12). Retrieved from Kennard Classical Junior Academy: http://kennardcja.com/index.php?p=2_2_History

Literacy Statistics. (2012, March 12). Retrieved from Begin to Read: http://www.begintoread.com/research/literacystatistics.html

Marian Wright Edelman Quotes. (2012, May 7). Retrieved from ThinkExist.com: http://thinkexist.com/quotation/the_challenge_of_social_justice_is_to_evoke_a/339121.html

Marva N. Collins Biography. (2012, March 12). Retrieved from Marva Collins Seminars, Inc. : http://www.marvacollins.com/biography.html

Maslow's Hierarchy of Needs. (2012, March 12). Retrieved from Wikipedia: http://en.wikipedia.org/wiki/Maslow%27s_hierarchy_of_needs

Pine Lawn Elementary School. (2012, March 12). Retrieved from Education.com, Inc. : http://www.education.com/schoolfinder/us/missouri/st-louis/pine-lawn-elementary/#/

Pittsburg Vann K-5 School. (2012, March 12). Retrieved from Local School Directory: http://www.localschooldirectory.com/public-school/345352287/PA

Anderson, T. C. (2004). *Closing the Achievement Gap: Reaching and Teaching High Poverty Learners: 101 Top Strategies to Help High Poverty Learners Succeed*. Lincoln: iUniverse.

Aronson, J. (2004). The Threat of Stereotype. *Educational Leadership*,

14-19.

Bambrick-Santoyo, P. (2010). *Driven by Data*. San Francisco: Jossey-Bass.

Barton, P. E. (2004). Why Does the Gap Persist? *Educational Leadership*, 8-13.

Bernhardt, V. L. (2004). *Data Analysis for Continous School Improvement*. Larchmont: Eye on Education Inc. .

Davenport, P., & Anderson, G. (2002). *Closing the Achievement Gap: No Excuses*. Houston: APQC Publications.

Draper, B. (2011, January 26). *Study: Missouri has nation's top black homicide rate*. Retrieved from The Missourian: http://www.columbiamissourian.com/stories/2011/01/26/study-mo-has-nations-top-black-homicide-rate/

DuFour, R., DuFour, R., & Eaker, R. (2008). *Revising Professional Learning Communities at Work: New Insights for Improving Schools*. Bloomington: Solution Tree Press.

DuFour, R., DuFour, R., Eaker, R., & Karhanek, G. (2004). *Whatever It Takes: How Professional Learning Communities Respond When Kids Don't Learn* . Bloomington: National Educational Service.

Goldberger, S., & Bayerl, K. (2008). *Beating the Odds:The Real Challenges Behind the Math*. Jobs for the Future.

Gurian, M., & Stevens, K. (2004). With Boys and Girls in Mind. *Educational Leadership*, 21-26.

Hemphill, F., & Vanneman, A. (2011). *Achievement Gaps: How Hispanic and White Students in Public Schools Perform in Mathematics and Reading on the National Assessment of Educational Progress (NCES 2011-459)*. Washington, DC: National Center for Education Statistics, Institute of Education Sciences, U.S. Department of Education.

Jacobs, H. H. (2010). *Curriculm 21: Essential Education For a Changing World*. Alexandria: ASCD.

Jensen, E. (2009). *Teaching With Poverty in Mind*. Alexandria: ASCD .

Jerald, C. D. (2006). *School Culture: "The Hidden Curriculum"*. Washington, DC: The Center for Comprehensive School Reform and Improvement.

Kirst, M. (2004). The High School/College Disconnect. *Educational Leadership*, 51-55.

Landsman, J. (2004). Confronting the Racism of Low Expectations. *Educational Leadership*, 28-32.

Lemov, D. (2010). *Teach Like a Champion*. San Francisco: Jossey-Bass.

McKensey and Company. (2009). *The Economic Impact of the Achievement Gap in America's Schools*.

Perry, T., Steele, C., & Hillard III, A. (2003). *Young Gifted and Black: Promoting High Achievement Among African American Students*. Boston: Beacon Press.

Reeves, D. B. (2003). *High Performance in High Poverty Schools: 90/90/90 and Beyond*. Center for Performance Assessment.

Reeves, D. B. (2009). *Leading Change in Your School*. Alexandria: ASCD.

Rothstein, R. (2004). The Achievement Gap: A Broader Picture. *Educational Leadership*, 40-43.

Vanneman, A., Hamilton, L., Baldwin Anderson, J., & Rahman, T. (2009). *Achievement Gaps: How Black and White Students in Public Schools Perform in Mathematics and Reading on the National Assessment of Educational Progress, (NCES 2009-455)*. Washington, DC: National Center for Education Statistics, Institute of Education Sciences, U.S. Department of Education.

Weber, K. (2010). *Waiting for "SUPERMAN"*. New York: PublicAffairs.

Williams, B. (2003). *Closing the Achievement Gap*. Alexandria: ASCD.

CPSIA information can be obtained
at www.ICGtesting.com
Printed in the USA
FFOW05n0601300617